THE LITTLE
MANX NATION

By
Hall Caine

The Little Manx Nation by Hall Caine

This edition © 2013 Camrose Media Ltd.

ISBN: 978-1-907945-54-0

Published 2013 by:
Lily Publications Ltd, PO Box 33, Ramsey, Isle of Man IM99 4LP.

To the
Reverend T. E. Brown, M.A.

You see what I send you—my lectures at the Royal Institution in the Spring. In making a little book of them I have thought it best to leave them as they were delivered with all the colloquialisms that are natural to spoken words frankly exposed to cold print. This does not help them to any particular distinction as literature, but perhaps it lends them an ease and familiarity which may partly atone to you and to all good souls for their plentiful lack of dignity. I have said so often that I am not an historian, that I ought to add that whatever history lies hidden here belongs to Train, our only accredited chronicler, and, even at the risk of bowing too low, I must needs protest, in our north-country homespun, that he shall have the pudding if he will also take the pudding-bag, You know what I mean. At some points our history—especially our early history—is still so vague, so dubious, so full of mystery. It is all the fault of little Mannanan, our ancient Manx magician, who enshrouded our island in mist. Or should I say it is to his credit, for has he not left us through all time some shadowy figures to fight about, like "rael, thrue, reg'lar" Manxmen? As for the stories, the "yarns" that lie like flies—like blue-bottles, like bees, I trust not like wasps—in the amber of the history, you will see that they are mainly my own. On second thought it occurs to me that maybe they are mainly yours. Let us say that they are both yours and mine, or perhaps, if the world finds anything good in them, any humour, any pathos, any racy touches of our rugged people, you will permit me to determine their ownership in the way of this paraphrase of Coleridge's doggerel version of the two Latin hexameters—

> "They're mine and they are likewise yours,
> But an if that will not do,
> Let them be mine, good friend! for I
> Am the poorer of the two."

Hawthorns, Keswick,
June 1891.

Sir Thomas Henry Hall Caine CH, KBE

CONTENTS

THE LITTLE MANX NATION

—•—

THE STORY OF THE MANX KINGS

THERE are just two ideas which are associated in the popular imagination with the first thought of the Isle of Man. The one is that Manxmen have three legs, and the other that Manx cats have no tails. But whatever the popular conception, or misconception, of Man and its people, I shall assume that what you ask from me is that simple knowledge of simple things which has come to me by the accident of my parentage. I must confess to you at the outset that I am not much of a hand at grave history. Facts and figures I cannot expound with authority. But I know the history of the Isle of Man, can see it clear, can see it whole, and perhaps it will content you if I can show you the soul of it and make it to live before you. In attempting to traverse the history I feel like one who carries a dark lantern through ten dark centuries. I turn the bull's eye on this incident and that, take a peep here and there, a white light now, and then a blank darkness. Those ten centuries are full of lusty fights, victories, vanquishments, quarrels, peace-making, shindies big and little, rumpus solemn and ridiculous, clouds of dust, regal dust, political dust, and religious dust—you know the way of it. But beneath it all and behind it all lies the real, true, living human heart of Manxland. I want to show it to you, if you will allow me to spare the needful time from facts and figures. It will get you close to Man and its people, and it is not to be found in the history books.

ISLANDERS

And now, first, we Manxmen are islanders. It is not
everybody who lives on an island that is an islander. You
know what I mean. I mean by an islander one whose daily
life is affected by the constant presence of the sea. This is
possible in a big island if it is far enough away from the rest
of the world, Iceland, for example, but it is inevitable in a little
one. The sea is always present with Manxmen. Everything
they do, everyrthing they say, gets the colour and shimmer
of the sea. The sea goes into their bones, it comes out at their
skin. Their talk is full of it. They buy by it, they sell by it, they
quarrel by it, they fight by it, they swear by it, they pray by it.
Of course they are not conscious of this. Only their
degenerate son, myself to wit, a chiel among them takin'
notes, knows how the sea exudes from the Manxmen. Say
you ask if the Governor is at home. If he is not, what is the
answer? "He's not on the island, sir." You inquire for the best
hotel. "So-and-so is the best hotel on the island, sir." You go
to a Manx fair and hear a farmer selling a cow. "Aw," says he,
"she's a ter'ble gran' craythuer for milkin', sir, and for butter
maybe there isn' the lek of her on the island, sir." Coming out
of church you listen to the talk of two old Manxwomen
discussing the preacher. "Well, well, ma'am, well, well! Aw,
the voice at him and the prayers! and the beautiful texe!
There isn' the lek of him on the island at all, at all!" Always
the island, the island, the island, or else the boats, and going
out to the herrings. The sea is always present. You feel it, you
hear it, you see it, you can never forget it. It dominates you.
Manxmen are all sea-folk.

You will think this implies that Manxmen stick close to
their island. They do more than that. I will tell you a story.
Five years ago I went up into the mountains to seek an old
Manx bard, last of a race of whom I shall have something to

tell you in their turn. All his life he had been a poet. I did not gather that he had read any poetry except his own. Up to seventy he had been a bachelor. Then this good Boaz had lit on his Ruth and married, and had many children. I found him in a lonely glen, peopled only in story, and then by fairies. A bare hill side, not a bush in sight, a dead stretch of sea in front, rarely brightened by a sail. I had come through a blinding hail-storm. The old man was sitting in the chimney nook, a little red shawl round his head and knotted under his chin. Within this aureole his face was as strong as Savonarola's, long and gaunt, and with skin stretched over it like parchment. He was no hermit, but a farmer, and had lived on that land, man and boy, nearly ninety years. He had never been off the island, and had strange notions of the rest of the world. Talked of England, London, theatres, palaces, king's entertainments, evening parties. He saw them all through the mists of rumour, and by the light of his Bible. He had strange notions, some of them bad shots for the truth, some of them startlingly true. I dare not tell you what they were. A Royal Institution audience would be aghast. They had, as a whole, a strong smell of sulphur. But the old bard was not merely an islander, he belonged to his land more than his land belonged to him. The fishing town nearest to his farm was Peel, the great fishing centre on the west coast. It was only five miles away. I asked how long it was since he had been there? "Fifteen years," he answered. The next nearest town was the old capital, on the east coast, Castletown, the home of the Governor, of the last of the Manx lords, the place of the Castle, the Court, the prison, the garrison, the College. It was just six miles away. How long was it since he had been there? "Twenty years." The new capital, Douglas, the heart of the island, its point of touch with the world, was nine miles away. How long since he had been in Douglas? "Sixty years," said the old bard. God bless him, the sweet, dear old soul! Untaught, narrow, self-centred, bred on his byre like his bullocks, but keeping his soul alive for all that, caring not a ha'porth for the things of the world, he was a true Manxman, and I'm proud of him. One thing I have to thank him for. But for him, and the like of him, we should not be here to-day. It is not the cultured Manxman, the Manxman that goes to the ends of the earth, that makes the Manx nation valuable to study. Our race is what it is by virtue of the Manxman who has had no life outside Man, and so has kept alive our language, our customs, our laws and our patriarchal Constitution.

OUR ISLAND

It lies in the middle of the Irish Sea, at about equal distances from England, Ireland, Scotland, and Wales. Seen from the sea it is a lovely thing to look upon. It never fails to bring me a thrill of the heart as it comes out of the distance. It lies like a bird on the waters. You see it from end to end, and from water's edge to topmost peak, often enshrouded in mists, a dim ghost on a grey sea; sometimes purple against the setting sun. Then as you sail up to it, a rugged rocky coast, grand in its beetling heights on the south and west, and broken into the sweetest bays everywhere. The water clear as crystal and blue as the sky in summer. You can see the shingle and the moss through many fathoms. Then mountains within, not in peaks, but round foreheads. The colour of the island is green and gold; its flavour is that of a nut. Both colour and flavour come of the gorse. This covers the mountains and moorlands, for, except on the north, the island has next to no trees. But O, the beauty and delight of it in the Spring! Long, broad stretches glittering under the sun with the gold of the gorse, and all the air full of the nutty perfume. There is nothing like it in the world. Then the glens, such fairy spots, deep, solemn, musical with the slumberous waters, clad in dark mosses, brightened by the red fuchsia. The fuchsia is everywhere where the gorse is not. At the cottage doors, by the waysides, in the gardens. If the gorse should fail the fuchsia might even take its place on the mountains. Such is Man, but I am partly conscious that it is Man as seen by a Manxman. You want a drop of Manx blood in you to see it aright. Then you may go the earth over and see grander things a thousand times, things more sublime and beautiful, but you will come back to Manxland and tramp the Mull Hills in May, long hour in, and long hour out, and look at the flowering gorse and sniff its flavour, or lie by the chasms and listen to the screams of the sea- birds, as they whirl and dip and dart and skim over the Sugar-loaf Rock, and you'll say after all that God has smiled on our little island, and that it is the fairest spot in His beautiful world, and, above all, that it is *ours*.

THE NAME OF OUR ISLAND

This is a matter in dispute among philologists and I am no authority. Some say that Caesar meant the Isle of Man when he spoke of Mona; others say he meant Anglesea. The present name is modern. So is Ellan Vannin, its Manx equivalent. In the Icelandic Sagas the island is called Mön. Elsewhere it is called Eubonia. One historian thinks the island derives its name from Mannin—*in* being an old Celtic word for island, therefore Meadhon-in (pronounced Mannin) would signify: The middle island. That definition requires that the Manxman had no hand in naming Man. He would never think of describing its geographical situation on the sea. Manxmen say the island got its name from a mythical personage called Mannanan-Beg-Mac-y-Learr, Little

Mannanan, son of Learr. This man was a sort of Prospero, a magician, and the island's first ruler. The story goes that if he dreaded an enemy he would enshroud the island in mist, "and that by art magic." Happy island, where such faith could ever exist! Modern science knows that mist, and where it comes from.

OUR HISTORY

It falls into three periods, first, a period of Celtic rule, second of Norse rule, third of English dominion. Manx history is the history of surrounding nations. We have no Sagas of our own heroes. The Sagas are all of our conquerors. Save for our first three hundred recorded years we have never been masters in our own house. The first chapter of our history has yet to be written. We know we were Celts to begin with, but how we came we have never learnt, whether we walked dry-shod from Wales or sailed in boats from Ireland. To find out the facts of our early history would be like digging up the island of Prospero. Perhaps we had better leave it alone. Ten to one we were a gang of political exiles. Perhaps we left our country for our country's good. Be it so. It was the first and last time that it could be said of us.

KING ORRY

Early in the sixth century Man became subject to the kings and princes of Wales, who ruled from Anglesea. There were twelve of them in succession, and the last of them fell in the tenth century. We know next to nothing about them but their names. Then came the Vikings. The young bloods of Scandinavia had newly established their Norse kingdom in

Iceland, and were huckstering and sea roving about the Baltic and among the British Isles. They had been to the Orkneys and Shetlands, and Faröes, perhaps to Ireland, certainly to the coast of Cumberland, making Scandinavian settlements everywhere. So they came to Mön early in the tenth century, led by one Orry, or Gorree. Some say this man was nothing but a common sea-rover. Others say he was a son of the Danish or Norwegian monarch. It does not matter much. Orry had a better claim to regard than that of the son of a great king. He was himself a great man. The story of his first landing is a stirring thing. It was night, a clear, brilliant, starry night, all the dark heavens lit up. Orry's ships were at anchor behind him; and with his men he had touched the beach, when down came the Celts to face him, and to challenge him. They demanded to know where he came from. Then the red-haired sea-warrior pointed to the milky way going off towards the North. "That is the way of my country," he answered. The Celts went down like one man in awe before him. He was their born king. It is what the actors call a fine moment. Still, nobody has ever told us how Orry and the Celts understood one another, speaking different tongues. Let us not ask.

King Orry had come to stay, and sea-warriors do not usually bring their women over tempestuous seas. So the Norsemen married the Celtic women, and from that union came the Manx people. Thus the Manxman to begin with was half Norse, half Celt. He is much the same still. Manxmen usually marry Manx women, and when they do not, they often marry Cumberland women. As the Norseman settled in Cumberland as well as in Man the race is not seriously affected either way. So the Manxman, such as he is, taken all the centuries through, is thoroughbred.

Now what King Orry did in the Isle of Man was the greatest work that ever was done there. He established our Constitution. It was on the model of the Constitution just established in Iceland. The government was representative and patriarchal. The Manx people being sea-folk, living by the sea, a race of fishermen and sea-rovers, he divided the island into six ship-shires, now called Sheadings. Each ship-shire elected four men to an assemblage of law-makers. This assemblage, equivalent to the Icelandic Logretta, was called the House of Keys. There is no saying what the word means. Prof. Rhys thinks it is derived from the Manx name *Kiare-as-Feed*, meaning the four-and-twenty. Train says the representatives were called Taxiaxi signifying pledges or hostages, and consequently were styled Keys. Vigfusson's theory was that Keys is from the Norse word *Ketse*, or chosen men. The common Manx notion, the idea familiar to my own boyhood, is, that the twenty-four members of the House of Keys are the twenty-four material keys whereby the closed doors of the law are unlocked. But besides the sea-folk of the ship-shires King Orry remembered the Church. He found it on the island at his coming, left it where he found it, and gave it a voice in the government. He established a Tynwald Court, equivalent to the Icelandic All Moot, where Church and State sat together. Then he appointed two law-men, called Deemsters, one for the north and the other for the south. These were equivalent to his Icelandic Lögsögumadur, speaker of the law and judge of all offences. Finally, he caused to be built an artificial Mount of Laws, similar in its features to the Icelandic Logberg at Thingvellir. Such was the machinery of the Norse Constitution which King Orry established in Man. The working of it was very simple. The House of Keys, the people's delegates, discussed all questions of interest to the people, and sent up its desires to the Tynwald Court. This assembly of people and Church in joint session assented, and the desires of the people became Acts of Tynwald. These Acts were submitted to the King. Having obtained the King's sanction they were promulgated on the

Tynwald Hill on the national day in the presence of the nation. The scene of that promulgation of the laws was stirring and impressive. Let me describe it.

THE TYNWALD

Perhaps there were two Tynwald Hills in King Orry's time, but I shall assume that there was one only. It stood somewhere about midway in the island. In the heart of a wide range of hill and dale, with a long valley to the south, a hill to the north, a table-land to the east, and to the west the broad Irish Sea. Not, of course, a place to be compared with the grand and gloomy valley of the Logberg, where in a vast amphitheatre of dark hills and great jökulls tipped with snow, with deep chasms and yawning black pits, one's heart stands still. But the place of the Manx Tynwald was an impressive spot. The Hill itself was a circular mount cut into broad steps, the apex being only a few feet in diameter. About it was a flat grass plot. Near it, just a hundred and forty yards away, connected with the mount by a beaten path, was a chapel. All around was bare and solitary, perhaps as bleak and stark as the lonely plains of Thingvellir.

Such was the scene. Hither came the King and his people on Tynwald Day. It fell on the 24th of June, the first of the seven days of the Icelandic gathering of the Althing. What occurred in Iceland occurred also in Man. The King with his Keys and his clergy gathered in the chapel. Thence they passed in procession to the law-rock. On the top round of the Tynwald the King sat on a chair and faced to the east. His sword was held before him, point upwards. His barons and beneficed men, his deemsters, knights, esquires, coroners, and yeomen, stood on the lower steps of the mount. On the grass plot beyond the people were gathered in crowds. Then the work of the day began. The coroners proclaimed a warning. No man should make disturbance at Tynwald on pain of death. Then the Acts of Tynwald were read or recited aloud by the deemsters; first in the language of the laws, and next in the language of the people. After other formalities the procession of the King returned to the chapel, where the laws were signed and attested, and so the annual Tynwald ended.

Now this primitive ceremonial, begun by King Orry early in the tenth century, is observed to this day. On Midsummer-day of this year of grace a ceremony similar in all its essentials will be observed by the present Governor, his Keys, clergy, deemsters, coroners, and people, on or near the same spot. It is the old Icelandic ordinance, but it has gone from Iceland. The year 1800 saw the last of it on the lava law-rock of Thingvellir. It is gone from every other Norse kingdom founded by the old sea-rovers among the Western Isles. Manxmen alone have held on to it. Shall we also let it go? Shall we laugh at it as a bit of mummery that is useless in an age of books and newspapers, and foolish and pompous in days of frock-coats and chimney-pot hats? I think not. We cannot afford to lose it. Remember, it is the last visible sign of our independence as a nation. It is our hand-grasp with the past. Our little nation is the only Norse nation now on earth that can shake hands with the days of the Sagas, and the Sea-Kings. Then let him who will laugh at our primitive ceremonial. It is the badge of our ancient liberty, and we need not envy the man who can look on it unmoved.

THE LOST SAGA

Of King Orry himself we learn very little. He was not only the first of our kings, but also the greatest. We may be sure of that; first, by what we know; and next, by what we do not know. He was a conqueror, and yet we do not learn that he ever attempted to curtail the liberties of his subjects. He found us free men, and did not try to make us slaves. On the contrary, he gave us a representative Constitution, which has lasted a thousand years. We might call him our Manx King Alfred, if the indirections of history did not rather tempt us to christen him our Manx King Lear. His Saga has never been written, or else it is lost. Would that we could recover it! Oh, that imagination had the authority of history to vitalise the old man and his times! I seem to see him as he lived. There are hints of his character in his laws, that are as stage directions, telling of the entrances and exits of his people, though the drama of their day is gone. For example, in that preliminary warning of the coroner at Tynwald, there is a clause which says that none shall "bawl or quarrel or lye or lounge or sit." Do you not see what that implies? Again, there is another clause which forbids any man, "on paine of life and lyme," to make disturbance or stir in the time of Tynwald, or any murmur or rising in the king's presence. Can you not read between the lines of that edict? Once more, no inquest of a deemster, no judge or jury, was necessary to the death-sentence of a man who rose against the king or his governor on his seat on Tynwald. Nobody can miss the meaning of that. Once again, it was a common right of the people to present petitions at Tynwald, a common privilege of persons unjustly punished to appeal against judgment, and a common prerogative of outlaws to ask at the foot of the Tynwald Mount on Tynwald Day for the removal of their outlawry. All these old rights and regulations came from Iceland, and by the help of the Sagas it needs no special imagination to make the scenes of their action live again. I seem to see King Orry sitting on his chair on the Tynwald with his face towards the east. He has long given up sea-roving. His long red hair is become grey or white. But the old lion has the muscles and fiery eye of the warrior still. His deemsters and barons are about him, and his people are on the sward below. They are free men; they mean to have their rights, both from him and from each other. Disputes run high, there are loud voices, mighty oaths, sometimes blows, fights, and terrific hurly-burlies. Then old Orry comes down with a great voice and a sword, and ploughs a way through the fighters and scatters them. No man dare lift his hand on the king. Peace is restored, and the king goes back to his seat.

Then up from the valley comes a woe-begone man in tatters, grim and gaunt and dirty, a famished and hunted wolf. He is an outlaw, has killed a man, is pursued in a blood-feud, and asks for relief of his outlawry. And so on and so on, a scene of rugged, lusty passions, hate and revenge, but also love and brotherhood; drinking, laughing, swearing, fighting, savage vices but also savage virtues, noble contempt of death, and magnificent self-sacrifice.

The chapter is lost, but we know what it must have been. King Orry was its hero. Our Manx Alfred, our Manx Arthur, our Manx Lear. Then room for him among our heroes! He must stand high.

THE MANX MACBETH

The line of Orry came to an end at the beginning of the eleventh century. Scotland was then under the sway of the tyrant Macbeth, and, oddly enough, a parallel tragedy to that of Duncan and his kinsman was being enacted in Man. A son of Harold the Black, of Iceland, Goddard Crovan, a mighty soldier, conquered the island and took the crown by treachery, coming first as a guest of the Manx king. Treachery breeds treachery, duplicity is a bad seed to sow for loyalty, and the Manx people were divided in their allegiance. About twenty years after Crovan's conquest the people of the south of the island took up arms against the people of the north, and the story goes that, when victory wavered, the women of the north rushed out to the help of their husbands, and so won the fight. For that day's work, the northern wives were given the right to half of all their husband's goods immovable, while the wives of the south had only a third. The last of the line of Goddard Crovan died in 1265, and so ended the dynasty of the Norsemen in Man. They had been three hundred years there. They found us a people of the race and language of the people of Ireland, and they left us Manxmen. They were our only true Manx kings, and when they fell, our independence as a nation ceased.

THE MANX GLO'STER

Then the first pretender to the throne was one Ivar, a murderer, a sort of Richard III, not all bad, but nearly all; said to possess virtues enough to save the island and vices enough to ruin it. The island was surrendered to Scotland by treaty with Norway, The Manx hated the Scotch. They knew them as a race of pirates. Some three centuries later there was one Cutlar MacCullock, whose name was a terror, so merciless were his ravages. Over the cradles of their infants the Manx mothers sang this song:—

> God keep the good corn, the sheep and the bullocks,
> From Satan, from sin and from Cutlar MacCullock.

Bad as Ivar was, the Scotch threatened to be worse. So the Manx, fearing that their kingdom might become a part of the kingdom of Scotland, supported Ivar. They were beaten. Ivar was a brave tiger, and died fighting.

SCOTCH AND ENGLISH DOMINION

Man was conquered, and the King of Scotland appointed a lieutenant to rule the island. But the Manx loved the Scotch no better as masters than as pirates, and they petitioned the English king, Edward I, to take them under his protection. He came, and the Scotch were driven out. But King Robert Bruce reconquered the island for the Scotch. Yet again the island fell to English dominion. This was in the time of Henry IV. It is a sorry story. Henry gave the island to the Earl of Salisbury. Salisbury sold it to one Sir William le Scroop. A copy of the deed of sale exists. It puts a Manxman's teeth on edge. "With all the right of being crowned with a golden crown." Scroop was beheaded by Henry, who confiscated his estate, and gave the island to the Earl of Northumberland. It is a silly inventory, but let us get through with it. Northumberland was banished, and finally Henry made a grant of the island to Sir John de Stanley. This was in 1407. Thus there had been four Kings of Man—not one of whom had, so far as I know, set foot on its soil—three grants of the island, and one miserable sale. Where the carcase is, there will the eagles be gathered together.

THE STANLEY DYNASTY

When the crown came to Sir John Stanley he was in no hurry to put it on. He paid no heed to his Manx subjects, and never saw his Manx kingdom. I dare say he thought the gift horse was something of a white elephant. No wonder if he did, for words could not exaggerate the wretched condition of the island and its people. The houses of the poor were hovels built of sod, with floors of clay, and sooty rafters of briar and straw and dried gorse. The people were hardly better fed than their beasts. So Stanley left the island alone. It will be interesting to mark how different was the mood of his children, and his children's children. The second Stanley went over to Man and did good work there. He promulgated our laws, and had them written down for the first time—they had hitherto been locked in the breasts of the deemsters in imitation of the practice of the Druids. The line of the Stanleys lasted more than three hundred years. Their rule was good for the island. They gave the tenants security of tenure, and the landowners an act of settlement. They lifted the material condition of our people, gave us the enjoyment of our venerable laws, and ratified our patriarchal Constitution. Honour to the Stanleys of the Manx dynasty! They have left a good mark on Man.

ILIAM DHOAN

And now I come to the one incident in modern Manx history which shares, with the three legs of Man and the Manx cat, the consciousness of everybody who knows anything about our island and its people. This is the incident of the betrayal of Man and the Stanleys to the Parliament in the time of Cromwell. It was a stirring drama, and though the curtain has long fallen on it, the dark stage is still haunted by the ghosts of its characters. Chief among these was William Christian, the Manxman called Iliam Dhoan, Brown William, a familiar name that seems to hint of a fine type of man. You will find him in "Peveril of the Peak." He is there mixed up with Edward Christian, a very different person, just as Peel Castle is mixed up with Castle Rushen, consciously no doubt, and with an eye to imaginative effects, for Scott had a brother in the Isle of Man who could have kept him from error if fact had been of any great consequence in the novelist's reckoning.

Christian was Receiver-General, a sort of Chancellor of

the Exchequer, for the great Earl of Derby. The Earl had faith in him, and put nearly everything under his command that fell within the province of his lordship. Then came the struggle with Rigby at Latham House, and the imprisonment of the Earl's six children by Fairfax. The Manx were against the Parliament, and subscribed £500, probably the best part of the money in the island, in support of the king. Then the Earl of Derby left the island with a body of volunteers, and in going away committed his wife to the care of Christian. You know what happened to him. He was taken prisoner in Lancashire, charged with bearing arms for Charles Stuart and holding the Isle of Man against the Commons, condemned, and executed at Bolton.

With the forfeiture of the Earl the lordship of the island was granted by Parliament to Lord Fairfax. He sent an army to take possession, but the Countess-Dowager still held the island. Christian commanded the Manx militia. At this moment the Manx people showed signs of disaffection. They suddenly remembered two grievances, one was a grievance of land tenure, the other was that a troop of soldiers was kept at free quarterage. I cannot but wish they had bethought them of both a little earlier. They formed an association, and broke into rebellion against the Countess-Dowager within eight days of the Earl's execution. Perhaps they did not know of the Earl's death, for news travelled slowly over sea in those days. But at least they knew of his absence. As a Manxman I am not proud of them.

During these eight days Mr. Receiver-General had begun to trim his sails. He had a lively wit, and saw which way things were going. Rumour says he was at the root of the secret association. Be that as it may, he carried the demands of the people to the Countess. She had no choice but to yield. The troops were disbanded. It was a bad victory.

A fortnight before, when her husband lay under his death

sentence, the Countess had offered the island in exchange for his life. So now Mr. Receiver-General used this act of love against her. He seized some of the forts, saying the Countess was selling the island to the Parliament. Then the army of the Parliament landed, and Christian straightaway delivered the island up to it, protesting that he had taken the forts on its behalf. Some say the Countess was imprisoned in the vaults of the Castle. Others say she had a free pass to England. So ended act one.

When the act-drop rose on act two, Mr. Receiver-General was in office under the Parliament. From the place of Receiver-General he was promoted to the place of Governor. He had then the money of the island under his control, and he used it badly. Deficits were found in his accounts. He fled to London, was arrested for a large debt, and clapped into the Fleet. Then the Commonwealth fell, the Dowager Countess went upstairs again, and Charles II restored the son of the great Earl to the lordship of Man. After that came the Act of Indemnity, a general pardon for all who had taken part against the royal cause. Thereupon Christian went back to the Isle of Man, was arrested on a charge of treason to the Countess-Dowager of Derby, pleaded the royal act of general pardon against all proceedings libelled against him, was tried by the House of Keys, and condemned to death. So ended act two.

Christian had a nephew, Edward Christian, who was one of the two deemsters. This man dissented from the voice of the court, and hastened to London to petition the king. Charles is said to have heard his plea, and to have sent an order to suspend sentence. Some say the order came too late; some say the Governor had it early enough and ignored it. At all events Christian was shot. He protested that he had never been anything but a faithful servant to the Derbys, and made a brave end. The place of his execution was Hango Hill, a bleak, bare stretch of land with the broad sea under it. The soldiers wished to bind Christian. "Trouble not yourselves for me," he said, "for I that dare face death in whatever shape he comes, will not start at your fire and bullets." He pinned a piece of white paper on his breast, and said: "Hit this, and you do your own work and mine." Then he stretched forth his arms as a signal, was shot through the heart, and fell. Such was the end of Brown William. He may have been a traitor, but he was no coward.

When the chief actor in the tragedy had fallen, King Charles appeared, as Fortinbras appears in "Hamlet," to make a review and a reckoning, and to take the spoils. He ordered the Governor, the remaining Deemsters, and three of the Keys to be brought before him, pronounced the execution of Christian to be a violation of his general pardon, and imposed severe penalties of fine and imprisonment. "The rest" in this drama has not been "silence." One long clamour has followed. Christian's guilt has been questioned, the legality of his trial has been disputed, the validity of Charles's censure of the judges has been denied. The case is a mass of tangle, as every case must be that stands between the two stools of the Royal cause and the Commonwealth. But I shall make bold to summarise the truth in a very few words:

First, that Christian was untrue to the house of Derby is as clear as noonday. If he had been their loyal servant he could never have taken office under the Parliament.

Second, though untrue to the Countess-Dowager, Christian could not be guilty of treason to her, because she had ceased to be the sovereign when her husband was executed. Fairfax was then the Lord of Man, and Christian was guilty of no treason to him.

Third, whether true or untrue to the Countess-Dowager, the act of pardon had nothing on earth to do with Christian, who was not charged with treason to King Charles, but to the

Manx reigning family. The Isle of Man was not a dominion of England, and if Charles's order had arrived before Christian's execution, the Governor, Keys, and Deemster would have been fully justified in shooting the man in defiance of the king.

I feel some diffidence in offering this opinion, but I can have none whatever in saying what I think of Christian. My fellow Manxmen are for the most part his ardent supporters. They affirm his innocence, and protest that he was a martyr-hero, declaring that at least he met his fate by asserting the rights of his countrymen. I shall not hesitate to say that I read the facts another way. This is how I see the man:

First, he was a servant of the Derbys, honoured, empowered, entrusted with the care of his mistress, the Countess, when his master, the Earl, left the island to fight for the king. Second, eight days after his master's fate, he rose in rebellion against his mistress and seized some of the forts of defence. Third, he delivered the island to the army of the Parliament, and continued to hold his office under it. Fourth, he robbed the treasury of the island and fled from his new masters, the Parliament. Fifth, when the new master fell he chopped round, became a king's man once more, and returned to the island on the strength of the general pardon. Sixth, when he was condemned to death he, who had held office under the Parliament, protested that he had never been anything but a faithful servant to the Derbys.

Such is Christian. *He* a hero! No, but a poor, sorry, knock-kneed time-server. A thing of rags and patches. A Manx Vicar of Bray. Let us talk of him as little as we may, and boast of him not at all. Man and Manxmen have no need ot him. No, thank God, we can tell of better men. Let us turn his picture to the wall.

THE ATHOL DYNASTY

The last of the Stanleys of the Manx dynasty died childless in 1735, and then the lordship of Man devolved by the female line on the second Duke of Athol by right of his grandmother, who was a daughter of the great Earl of Derby. There is little that is good to say of the Lords of the House of Athol except that they sold the island. Almost the first, and quite the best, thing they did on coming to Man, was to try to get out of it. Let us make no disguise of the clear truth. The Manx Athols were bad, and nearly everything about them was bad. Never was the condition of the island so abject as during their day. Never were the poor so poor. Never was the name of Manxman so deservedly a badge of disgrace. The chief dishonour was that of the Athols. They kept a swashbuckler court in their little Manx kingdom. Gentlemen of the type of Barry Lyndon overran it. Captain Macheaths, Jonathan Wilds, and worse, were masters of the island, which was now a refuge for debtors and felons. Roystering, philandering, gambling, fighting, such was the order of things. What days they had! What nights! His Grace of Athol was himself in the thick of it all. He kept a deal of company, chiefly rogues and rascals. For example, among his " lord captains" was one Captain Fletcher. This Blue Beard had a magnificent horse, to which, when he was merry, he made his wife, who was a religious woman, kneel down and say her prayers. The mother of my friend, the Reverend T. E. Brown, came upon the dead body of one of these Barry Lyndons, who had fallen in a duel, and the blue mark was on the white forehead, where the pistol shot had been. I remember to have heard of another Sir Lucius O'Trigger, whose body lay exposed in the hold of a fishing-smack, while a parson read the burial service from the quay. This was some artifice to prevent seizure for debt. Oh, these good old times, with their soiled and dirty splendours! There was no lively chronicler, no Pepys, no Walpole then, to give us a picture of the Court of these Kings of Man. What a picture it must have been! Can you not see it? The troops of gentlemen debtors from the Coffee Houses of London, with their periwigs, their canes, and fine linen; down on their luck, but still beruffled, besnuffed, and red-heeled. I can see them strutting with noses up, through old Douglas market-place on market morning, past the Manx folk in their homespun, their curranes and undyed stockings. Then out at Mount Murray, the home of the Athols, their imitations of Vauxhall, torches, dancings, bows and congas, bankrupt shows, perhaps, but the bankrupt Barrys making the best of them—one seems to see it all. And then again, their genteel quarrels—quarrels were easily bred in that atmosphere. "Sir, I have the honour to tell you that you are a pimp, lately escaped from the Fleet." "My lord, permit me to say that you lie, that you are the son of a lady, and were born in a sponging-house." Then out leapt the weapons, and presently two men were crossing swords under the trees, and by-and-by one of them was left under the moonlight, with the shadow of the leaves playing on his white face.

Poor gay dogs, they are dead! The page of their history is lost. Perhaps that is just as well. It must have been a dark page, maybe a little red too, even as blood runs red. You can see the scene of their revelries. It is an inn now. The walls seem to echo to their voices. But the tables they ate at are like themselves—worm-eaten. Good-bye to them! They have gone over the Styx.

SMUGGLING AND WRECKING

Meanwhile, what of the Manx people? Their condition was pitiful. An author who wrote fifty years after the advent of the Athols gives a description of such misery that one's flesh creeps as one reads it. Badly housed, badly clad, badly fed and hardly taught at all, the very poor were in a state of abjectness unfit for dogs. Treat men as dogs and they speedily acquire the habits of dogs, the vices of dogs, and none of their virtues. That was what happened to a part of the Manx people; they developed the instincts of dogs, while their masters, the other dogs, the gay dogs, were playing their bad game together. Smuggling became common on the coasts of Man. Spirits and tobacco were the goods chiefly smuggled, and the illicit trade rose to a great height. There was no way to check it. The island was an independent kingdom. My lord of Athol swept in the ill-gotten gains, and his people got what they could. It was a game of grab. Meantime the trade of the surrounding countries, England, Wales, and Ireland, was suffering grievously. The name of the island must have smelt strong in those days.

But there was a fouler odour than that of smuggling. Wrecking was not unknown. The island lent itself naturally to that evil work. The mists of Little Mannanan, son of Lear, did not forsake our island when Saint Patrick swept him out of it. They continued to come up from the south, and to conspire with the rapid currents from the north to drive ships on to our rocks. Our coasts were badly lighted, or lighted not at all. An open flare stuck out from a pole at the end of a pier was often all that a dangerous headland had to keep vessels away from it. Nothing was easier than for a fishing smack to run down pole and flare together, as if by accident, on returning to harbour. But there was a worse danger than bad lights, and that was false lights. It was so easy to set them.

Sometimes they were there of themselves, without evil intention of any human soul, luring sailors to their destruction. Then when ships came ashore it was so easy to juggle with one's conscience and say it was the will of God, and no bad doings of any man's. The poor sea-going men were at the bottom of the sea by this time, and their cargo was drifting up with the tide, so there was nothing to do but to take it. Such was the way of things. The Manxman could find his excuses. He was miserably poor, he had bad masters, smuggling was his best occupation, his coasts were indifferently lighted, ships came ashore of themselves—what was he to do? That the name of Manxman did not become a curse, an execration, and a reproach in these evil days of the Athols seems to say that behind all this wicked work there were splendid virtues doing noble duty somewhere. The real sap, the true human heart of Manxland, was somehow kept alive. Besides cut-throats in ruffles, and wreckers in homespun, there were true, sweet, simple-hearted people who would not sell their souls to fill their mouths.

Does it surprise you that some of all this comes within the memory of men still living? I am myself well within the period of middle life, and, though too young to touch these evil days, I can remember men and women who must have been in the thick of them. On the north of the island is Kirk Maughold Head, a bold, rugged headland going far out into the sea. Within this rocky foreland lie two bays, sweet coverlets of blue waters, washing a shingly shore under shelter of dark cliffs. One of these bays is called Port-y-Vullin, and just outside of it, between the mainland and the head, is a rock, known as the Carrick, a treacherous grey reef, visible at low water, and hidden at flood-tide. On the low *brews* of Port-y-Vullin stood two houses, the one a mill, worked by the waters coming down from the near mountain of Barrule, the other a weaver's cottage. Three weavers lived together there, all bachelors, and all old, and never a woman or child among them—Jemmy of eighty years, Danny of seventy, and Billy of sixty something. Year in, year out, they worked at their looms, and early or late, whenever you passed on the road behind, you heard the click of them. Fishermen coming back to harbour late at night always looked for the light of their windows. "Yander's Jemmy-Danny-Billy's," they would say, and steer home by that landmark. But the light which guided the native seamen misled the stranger, and many a ship in the old days was torn to pieces on the jagged teeth of that sea-lion, the Carrick. Then, hearing loud human cries above the shrieks of wind and wave, the three helpless old men would come tottering down to the beach, like three innocent witches, trembling and wailing, holding each other's hands like little children, and never once dreaming of what bad work the candles over their looms had done.

But there were those who were not so guileless. Among them was a sad old salt, whom I shall call Hommy-Billy-mooar, Tommy, son of big Billy. Did I know him, or do I only imagine him as I have heard of him? I cannot say, but nevertheless I see him plainly. One of his eyes was gone, and the other was badly damaged. His face was of stained mahogany, one side of his mouth turned up, the other side turned down, he could laugh and cry together. He was half landsman, tilling his own croft, half seaman, going out with the boats to the herrings. In his youth he had sailed on a smuggler, running in from Whitehaven with spirits. The joy of "the trade," as they called smuggling, was that a man could buy spirits at two shillings a gallon for sale on the island, and drink as much as he "plazed abooard for nothin'." When Hommy married, he lived in a house near the church, the venerable St. Maughold away on the headland, with its lonely churchyard within sound of the sea. There on tempestuous nights the old eagle looked out from his eyrie on the doings of the sea, over the back of the cottage of the old weavers to the Carrick. If anything came ashore he awakened his boys, scurried over to the bay, seized all they could carry, stole back home, hid his treasures in the thatch of the roof, or among the straw of the loft, went off to bed, and rose in the morning with an innocent look, and listened to the story of last night's doings with a face full of surprise. They say that Hommy carried on this work for years, and though many suspected, none detected him, not even his wife, who was a good Methodist. The poor woman found him out at last, and, being troubled with a conscience, she died, and Hommy buried her in Kirk Maughold churchyard, and put a stone over her with a good inscription. Then he went on as before. But one morning there was a mighty hue and cry. A ship had been wrecked on the Carrick, and the crew who were saved had seen some rascals carrying off in the darkness certain rolls of Irish cloth which they had thrown overboard. Suspicion lit on Hommy and his boys. Hommy was quite hurt. "Wrecking was it? Lord a-massy I To think, to think!" Revenue officers were to come to-morrow to search his house. Those rolls of Irish cloth were under the thatch, above the dry gorse stored up on the "lath" in his cowhouse. That night he carried them off to the churchyard, took up the stone from over his wife's grave, dug the grave open and put in the cloth. Next day his one eye wept a good deal while the officers of revenue made their fruitless search. "Aw well, well, did they think because a man was poor he had no feelings?" Afterwards he pretended to become a Methodist, and then he removed the cloth from his wife's grave because he had doubts about how she could rise in the resurrection with such a weight on her coffin. Poor old Hommy, he came to a bad end. He spent his last days in jail in Castle Rushen. A one-eyed mate of his told me he saw him there. Hommy was unhappy. He said "Castle Rushen wasn't no place for a poor man when he was gettin' anyways ould."

THE REVESTMENT

It is hardly a matter for much surprise that the British Government did what it could to curb the smuggling that was rife in Man in the days of the Athols. The bad work had begun in the days of the Derbys, when an Act was passed which authorised the Earl of Derby to dispose of his royalty and revenue in the island, and empowered the Lords of the Treasury to treat with him for the sale of it. The Earl would not sell, and when the Duke of Athol was asked to do so, he tried to put matters off. But the evil had by this time grown so grievously that the British Government threatened to strip the Duke without remuneration. Then he agreed to accept £70,000 as compensation for the absolute surrender of the island. He was also to have £2000 out of the Irish revenue, which, as well as the English revenue, was to benefit by the suppression of the clandestine trade. This was in exchange for some £6000 a year which was the Duke's Manx revenue, much of it from duties and customs paid in goods which were afterwards smuggled into England, Ireland, and Scotland. So much for his Grace of Athol. Of course the Manx people got nothing. The thief was punished, the receiver was enriched; it is the way of the world.

In our history of Man, we call this sweet transaction, which occurred in 1765, "The Revestment," meaning the revesting of the island in the crown of England. Our Manx people did not like it at all. I have heard a rugged old song on the subject sung at Manx inns:

> For the babes unborn shall rue the day
> When the Isle of Man was sold away;
> And there's ne'er an old wife that loves a dram
> But she will lament for the Isle of Man.

Clearly drams became scarce when "the trade" was put down. But, indeed, the Manx had the most strange fears and ludicrous sorrows. The one came of their anxiety about the fate of their ancient Constitution, the other came of their foolish generosity. They dreaded that the government of the island would be merged into that of England, and they imagined that because the Duke of Athol had been compelled to surrender, he had been badly treated. Their patriotism was satisfied when the Duke of Athol was made Governor-in-Chief under the English crown, for then it was clear that they were to be left alone; but their sympathy was moved to see him come back as servant who had once been lord. They had disliked the Duke of Athol down to that hour, but they forgot their hatred in sight of his humiliation, and when he landed in his new character, they received him with acclamations. I am touched by the thought of my countrymen's unselfish conduct in that hour; but I thank God I was not alive to witness it. I should have shrieked with laughter. The absurdity of the situation passes the limits even of a farce. A certain Duke, who had received £6000 a year, whereof a large part came of an immoral trade, had been to London and sold his interest in it for £70,000, because if he had not taken that, he would probably have got nothing. With thirteen years' purchase of his insecure revenue in his pocket, and £2000 a year promised, and his salary as Governor-in-Chief besides, he returns to the island where half the people are impoverished by his sale of the island, and nobody else has received a copper coin, and everybody is doomed to pay back interest on what the Duke has received! What is the picture? The Duke lands at the old jetty, and there his carriage is waiting to take him to the house, where he and his have kept swashbuckler courts, with troops of fine gentlemen debtors from London. The Manxmen forget everything except that his dignity is reduced. They unyoke his horses, get into his shafts, drag him through the streets, toss up their caps and cry hurrah! hurrah! One seems to see the Duke sitting there with his arms folded, and his head on his breast. He can't help laughing. The thing is too ridiculous. Oh, if Swift had been there to see it, what a scorching satire we should have had!

But the Athols soon spirited away their popularity. First they clamoured for a further sum on account of the lost revenues, and they got it. Then they tried to appropriate part of the income of the clergy. Again, they put members of their family into the bishopric, and one of them sold his tithes to a factor who tried to extort them by strong measures, which led to green crop riots. In the end, their gross selfishness, which thought of their own losses but forgot the losses of the people, raised such open marks of aversion in the island that they finally signified to the king their desire to sell all their remaining rights, their land and manorial rights. This they did in 1829, receiving altogether, for custom, revenue, tithes, patronage of the bishopric, and quit rents, the sum of £416,000. Such was the value to the last of the Athols of the Manx dynasty, of that little hungry island of the Irish Sea, which Henry IV gave to the Stanleys, and Sir John de Stanley did not think worth while to look at. So there was an end of the House of Athol. Exit the House of Athol! The play goes on without them.

HOME RULE

It might be said that with the final sale of 1829 the history of the Isle of Man came to a close. Since then we have been in the happy condition of the nation without a history. Man is now a dependency of the English crown. The crown is represented by a Lieutenant-Governor. Our old Norse Constitution remains. We have Home Rule, and it works well.

The Manx people are attached to the throne of England, and her Majesty has not more loyal subjects in her dominions. We are deeply interested in Imperial affairs, but we have no voice in them. I do not think we have ever dreamt of a day when we should send representatives to Westminster. Our sympathies as a nation are not altogether, I think, with the party of progress. We are devoted to old institutions, and hold fast to such of them as are our own. All this is, perhaps, what you would expect of a race of islanders with our antecedents.

Our social history has not been brilliant. I do not gather that the Isle of Man was ever Merry Man. Not even in its gayest days do we catch any note of merriment amid the rumpus of its revelries. It is an odd thing that woman plays next to no part whatever in the history of the island. Surely ours is the only national pie in which woman has not had a finger. In this respect the island justifies the ungallant reading of its name—it is distinctly the Isle of Man. Not even amid the glitter and gewgaws of our Captain Macheaths do you catch the glint of the gown of a Polly. No bevy of ladies, no merry parties, no pageants worthy of the name. No, our social history gives no idea of Merry Man.

Our civil history is not glorious. We are compelled to allow that it has no heroism in it. There has been no fight for principle, no brave endurance of wrong. Since the days of Orry, we have had nothing to tell in Saga, if the Sagaman were here. We have played no part in the work of the world. The great world has been going on for ten centuries without taking much note of us. We are a little nation, but even little nations have held their own. We have not.

One great king we have had, King Orry. He gave us our patriarchal Constitution, and it is a fine thing. It combines most of the best qualities of representative government. Its freedom is more free than that of some republics. The people seem to be more seen, and their voice more heard, than in any other form of government whose operation I have witnessed. Yet there is nothing noisy about our Home Rule. And this Constitution we have kept alive for a thousand years, while it has died out of every other Norse kingdom. That is, perhaps, our highest national honour. We may have played a timid part; we may have accepted rulers from anywhere; we may never have made a struggle for independence; and no Manxman may ever have been strong enough to stand up alone for his people. It is like our character that we have taken things easily, and instead of resisting our enemies, or throwing them from our rocky island into the sea, we have been law abiding under lawless masters and peaceful under oppression. But this one thing we have done: we have clung to our patriarchal Constitution, not caring a ha'p'orth who administered our laws so long as the laws were our own. That is something; I think it is a good deal. It means that through many changes undergone by the greater peoples of the world, we are King Orry's men still. Let me in a last word tell you a story which shows what that description implies.

ORRY'S SONS

On the west coast of the Isle of Man stands the town of Peel. It is a little fishing port, looking out on the Irish Sea. To the north of it there is a broad shore, to the south lies the harbour with a rocky headland called Contrary Head; in front—until lately divided from the mainland by a narrow strait—is a rugged island rock. On this rock stand the broken ruins of a castle. Peel Castle, and never did castle stand on a grander spot. The sea flows round it, beating on the jagged cliffs beneath, and behind it are the wilder cliffs of Contrary. In the water between and around Contrary contrary currents flow, and when the wind is high they race and prance there like an unbroken horse. It is a grand scene, but a perilous place for ships.

One afternoon in October of 1889 a Norwegian ship (strange chance!), the *St. George* (a name surely chosen by the Fates!), in a fearful tempest was drifting on to Contrary Head. She was labouring hard in the heavy sea, rearing, plunging, creaking, groaning,and driving fast through clamouring winds and threshing breakers on to the cruel, black, steep horns of rock. All Peel was down at the beach watching her. Flakes of sea-foam were flying around, and the waves breaking on the beach were scooping up the shingle and flinging it through the air like sleet.

Peel has a lifeboat, and it was got out. There were so many volunteers that the harbour-master had difficulties of selection. The boat got off; the coxswain was called Charlie Cain; one of his crew was named Gorry, otherwise Orry. It was a perilous adventure. The Norwegian had lost her masts, and her spars were floating around her in the snow-like surf. She was dangerous to approach, but the lifeboat reached her. Charlie cried out to the Norwegian captain: "How many of you?" The answer came back, "Twenty-two!" Charlie counted them as they hung on at the ship's side, and said: "I only see twenty-one; not a man shall leave the ship until you bring the odd one on deck." The odd one, a disabled man, had been left below to his fate. Now he was brought up, and all were taken aboard the lifeboat.

On landing at Peel there was great excitement, men cheering and women crying. The Manx women spotted a baby among the Norwegians, fought for it, one woman got it, and carried it off to a fire and dry clothing. It was the captain's wife's baby, and an hour afterwards the poor captain's wife, like a creature distracted, was searching for it all over the town. And to heighten the scene, reports said that at that tremendous moment a splendid rainbow spanned the bay from side to side. That ought to be true if it is not.

It was a brilliant rescue, but the moving part of the story is yet to tell. The Norwegian Government, touched by the splendid heroism of the Manxmen, struck medals for the lifeboat men and sent them across to the Governor. These medals were distributed last summer on the island rock within the ruins of old Peel Castle. Think of it! One thousand years before, not far from that same place, Orry the Viking came ashore from Denmark or Norway. And now his Manx sons, still bearing his very name, Orry, save from the sea the sons of the brethren he left behind, and down the milky way, whence Orry himself once came, come now to the Manxmen the thanks and the blessings of their kinsmen, Orry's father's children.

Such a story as this thrills one to the heart. It links Manxmen to the great past. What are a thousand years before it? Time sinks away, and the old sea-warrior seems to speak to us still through the surf of that storm at Peel.

THE STORY OF THE MANX BISHOPS

SOME years ago, in going down the valley of Foxdale, towards the mouth of Glen Rushen, I lost my way on a rough and unbeaten path under the mountain called Slieu Whallin. There I was met by a typical old Manx farmer, who climbed the hillside some distance to serve as my guide. "Aw, man," said he, "many a Sunday I've crossed these mountains in snow and hail together." I asked why on Sunday. "You see," said the old fellow, "I'm one of those men that have been guilty of what St. Paul calls the foolishness of preaching." It turned out that he was a local preacher to the Wesleyans, and that for two score years or more, in all seasons, in all weathers, every Sunday, year in, year out, he had made the journey from his farm in Foxdale to the western villages of Kirk Patrick, where his voluntary duty lay. He left me with a laugh and a cheery word. "Ask again at the cottage at the top of the brew," he shouted. "An ould widda lives there with her gel." At the summit of the hill, just under South Barrule, with Cronk-ny- arrey-Lhaa to the west, I came upon a disused lead mine, called the old Cross Vein, its shaft open save for a plank or two thrown across it, and filled with water almost to the surface of the ground. And there, under the lee of the roofless walls of the ruined engine-house, stood the tiny one-story cottage where I had been directed to inquire my way again. I knocked, and then saw the outer conditions of an existence about as miserable as the mind of man can conceive. The door was opened by a youngish woman, having a thin, white face, and within the little house an elderly woman was breaking scraps of vegetables into a pot that swung from a hook above a handful of turf fire, which burned on the ground. They were the widow and daughter. Their house consisted of two rooms, a living room and a sleeping closet, both open to the thatch, which was sooty with smoke. The floor was of bare earth, trodden hard and shiny. There was one little window in each apartment, but after the breakages of years, the panes were obscured by rags stuffed into the gaps to keep out the weather. The roof bore traces of damp, and I asked if the rain came into the house. "Och, yes, and bad, bad, bad!" said the elder woman. "*He* left us, sir, years ago." That was her way of saying that her husband was dead, and that since his death there had been no man to do an odd job about the place. The two women lived by working in the fields, at weeding, at planting potatoes, at thinning cabbages, and at the hay in its season. Their little bankrupt barn belonged to them, and it was all they had. In that they lived, or lingered, on the mountain top, a long stretch of bare hillside, away from any neighbour, alone in their poverty, with mountains before and behind, the broad grey sea, without ship or sail, down a gully to the west, nothing visible to the east save the smoke from the valley where lay the habitations of men, nothing audible anywhere but the deep rumble of the waves' bellow, or the chirp of the birds overhead, or, perhaps, when the wind was southerly, the church bells on Sunday morning. Never have I looked upon such lonely penury, and yet there, even there, these forlorn women kept their souls alive. "Yes," they said, "we're working when we can get the work, and trusting, trusting, trusting still."

I have lingered too long over this poor adventure of losing my way to Glen Rushen, but my little sketch may perhaps get you close to that side of Manx life whereon I wish to speak to-day. I want to tell the history of religion in Man, so far as we know it; and better, to my thinking, than a grave or solid disquisition on the ways and doings of Bishops or Spiritual Barons, are any peeps into the hearts and home lives of the Manx, which will show what is called the "innate religiosity" of the humblest of the people. To this end also, when I have discharged my scant duty to church history, or perhaps in the course of my hasty exposition of it, I shall dwell on some of those homely manners and customs, which, more than prayer-books and printed services, tell us what our fathers believed, what we still believe, and how we stand towards that other life, that inner life, that is not concerned with what we eat and what we drink, and wherewithal we shall be clothed.

THE DRUIDS

And now, just as the first chapter of our Manx civil history is lost, so the first chapter of our church history is lost. That the Druids occupied the island seems to some people to be clear from many Celtic names and some remains, such as we are accustomed to call Druidical, and certain customs still observed. Perhaps worthy of a word is the circumstance that in the parish where the Bishop now lives, and has always lived. Kirk Michael, there is a place called by a name which in the Manx signifies Chief Druid. Strangely are the faiths ot the ages linked together.

CONVERSION TO CHRISTIANITY

We do not know, with any certainty, at what time the island was converted to Christianity. The accepted opinion is that Christianity was established in Man by St. Patrick about the middle of the fifth century. The story goes that the Saint of Ireland was on a voyage thither from England, when a storm cast him ashore on a little islet on the western coast of Man. This islet was afterwards called St. Patrick's Isle. St. Patrick built his church on it. The church was rebuilt eight centuries later within the walls of a castle which rose on the same rocky site. It became the cathedral church of the island. When the

Norwegians came they renamed the islet Holm Isle. Tradition
says that St. Patrick's coming was in the time of Mannanan,
the magician, our little Manx Prospero. It also says that St.
Patrick drove Mannanan away, and that St. Patrick's successor,
St. Germain, followed up the good work of exterminating evil
spirits by driving out of the island all venomous creatures
whatever. We sometimes bless the memory of St. Germain,
and wish he would come again.

THE EARLY BISHOPS OF MAN

After St. Germain came St. Maughold. This Bishop was a sort
of transfigured Manx Caliban. I trust the name does him no
wrong. He had been an Irish prince, had lived a bad, gross
life as a robber at the head of a band of robbers, had been
converted by St. Patrick, and, resolving to abandon the
temptations of the world, had embarked on the sea in a
wicker boat without oar or helm. Almost he had his will at
once, but the north wind, which threatened to remove him
from the temptations of this world, cast him ashore on the
north of the Isle of Man. There he built his church, and the
rocky headland whereon it stands is still known by his name.
High on the craggy cliff-side, looking towards the sea, is a
seat hewn out of the rock. This is called St. Maughold's Chair.
Not far away there is a well which is supposed to possess
miraculous properties. It is called St. Maughold's Well. Thus
tradition has perpetuated the odour of his great sanctity,
which is the more extraordinary in a variation of his legend,
which says that it was not after his conversion, and in
submission to the will of God, that he put forth from Ireland
in his wicker boat, but that he was thrust out thus, with hands
and feet bound, by way of punishment for his crimes as a
captain of banditti.

But if Maughold was Caliban in Ireland, he was more than Prospero in Man. Rumour of his piety went back to Ireland, and St. Bridget, who had founded a nunnery at Kildare, resolved on a pilgrimage to the good man's island. She crossed the water, attended by her virgins, called her daughters of fire, founded a nunnery near Douglas, worked miracles there, touched the altar in testimony of her virginity, whereupon it grew green and flourished. This, if I may be pardoned the continued parallel, is our Manx Miranda. And indeed it is difficult to shake off the idea that Shakespeare must have known something of the early story of Man, its magicians and its saints. We know the perfidy of circumstance, the lying tricks that fact is always playing with us, too well and painfully to say anything of the kind with certainty. But the angles of resemblance are many between the groundwork of the "Tempest" and the earliest of Manx records. Mannanan-beg-Mac-y-Lear, the magician who surrounded the island with mists when enemies came near in ships; Maughold, the robber and libertine, bound hand and foot, and driven ashore in a wicker boat; and then Bridget, the virgin saint. Moreover, the stories of Little Mannanan, of St. Patrick, and of St. Maughold were printed in Manx in the sixteenth century. Truly that is not enough, for, after all, we have no evidence that Shakespeare, who knew everything, knew Manx. But then Man has long been famous for its seamen. We had one of them at Trafalgar, holding Nelson in his arms when he died. The best days, or the worst days—which?—of the trade of the West Coast of Africa saw Manx captains in the thick of it. Shall I confess to you that in the bad days of the English slave trade the four merchant-men that brought the largest black cargo to the big human auction mart at the Goree Piazza at Liverpool were commanded by four Manxmen! They were a sad quartet. One of them had only one arm and an iron hook; another had only one arm and one eye; a third had only one leg and a stump; the fourth was covered with scars from the iron of the chains of a slave which he had worn twelve months at Barbadoes. Just about enough humanity in the four to make one complete man. But with vigour enough, fire enough, heart enough—I daren't say soul enough—in their dismembered old trunks to make ten men apiece; born sea-rovers, true sons of Orry, their blood half brine. Well, is it not conceivable that in those earlier days of treasure seeking, when Elizabeth's English captains were spoiling the Spaniard in the Indies, Manx sailors were also there? If so, why might not Shakespeare, who must have ferreted out many a stranger creature, have found in some London tavern an old Manx sea-dog, who could tell him of the Manx Prospero, the Manx Caliban, and the Manx Miranda?

But I have rambled on about my sailors; I must return to my Bishops. They seem to have been a line of pious, humble, charitable, godly men at the beginning. Irishmen, chiefly, living the lives of hermits and saints. Apparently they were at first appointed by the people themselves. Would it be interesting to know the grounds of selection? One was selected for his sanctity, a natural qualification, but another was chosen because he had a pleasant face, and a fine portly figure; not bad qualifications, either. Thus things went on for about a hundred years, and, for all we know, Celtic Bishops and Celtic people lived together in their little island in peace, hearing nothing of the loud religious hubbub that was disturbing Europe.

BISHOPS OF THE WELSH DYNASTY

Then came the rule of the Welsh kings, and, though we know but little with certainty, we seem to realise that it brought great changes to the religious life of Man. The Church began to possess itself of lands; the baronial territories of the island fell into the hands of the clergy; the early Bishops became Barons. This gave the Church certain powers of government. The Bishops became judges, and as judges they possessed great power over the person of the subject. Sometimes they stood in the highest place of all, being also Governor to the Welsh Kings. Then they were called Sword-Bishops. Their power at such times, when the crosier and sword were in the two hands of one man, must have been portentous, and even terrible. We have no records that picture what came of that. But it is not difficult to imagine the condition. The old order of things had passed away. The hermit-saints, the saintly hermits, had gone, and in their place were monkish barons, living in abbeys and monasteries, whipping the poor bodies of their people, as well as comforting their torn hearts, fattening on broad lands, praying each with his lips: "Give us this day our daily bread," but saying each to his soul: "Soul, thou hast much goods laid up for many years; take thine ease: eat, drink, and be merry."

BISHOPS OF THE NORSE DYNASTY

Little as we know of these times, we see that things must have come to a pretty pass, for when the Scandinavian dynasty came in the ecclesiastical authorities were forbidden to exercise civil control over any subjects of the king that were not also the tenants of their own baronies. So the Bishops were required to confine themselves to keeping their own house in order. The Norse Constitution established in Man by King Orry made no effort to overthrow the Celtic Church founded by St. Patrick, and corrupted by his Welsh successors, but it curtailed its liberties, and reduced its dignity. It demanded as an act of fealty that the Bishop or

chief Baron should hold the stirrup of the King's saddle, as
he mounted his horse at Tynwald. But it still suffered the
Bishop and certain of his clergy to sit in the highest court of
the legislature. The Church ceased to be purely Celtic; it
became Celto-Scandinavian, otherwise Manx. It was under
the Archbishop of Drontheim for its Metropolitan, and its
young clergy were sent over to Drontheim to be educated. Its
revenues were apportioned after the most apostolic manner;
one-third of the tithes to the Bishop for his maintenance, the
support of his courts, his churches, and (miserable
conclusion!) his prisons; one-third to the priests, and the
remaining third to the relief of the poor and the education of
youth. It is a curious and significant fact that when the
Reformation came the last third was seized by the lord. Good
old lordly trick, we know it well!

SODOR AND MAN

The Bishopric of the island was now no longer called the
Bishopric of Man, but Sodor and Man. The title has given rise
to much speculation. One authority derives it from
Soterenssis a name given by Danish writers to the western
islands, and afterwards corrupted to Soderensis. Another
authority derives it from *Sudreyjas*, signifying in the
Norwegian the Southern Isles. A third derives it from the
Greek *Soter*, Saviour, to whose name the cathedral of Iona
was dedicated. And yet a fourth authority derives it from the
supposed third name of the little islet rock called variously
Holm Isle, Sodor, Peel, and St. Patrick's Isle, whereon St.
Patrick or St. Germain built his church. I can claim no right
to an opinion where these good doctors differ, and shall
content myself with saying that the balance of belief is in
favour of the Norwegian derivation, which offers this

THE LITTLE MANX NATION

explanation of the title of Bishop of Sodor and Man, that the Isle of Man was not included by the Norsemen in the southern cluster of islands called the Sudereys, and that the Bishop was sometimes called the Bishop of Man and the Isles, and sometimes Bishop of the Sudereys and the Isle of Man. Only one warning note shall I dare, as an ignorant layman, to strike on that definition, and it is this: that the title of Bishop of Sodor dates back to the seventh century certainly, and that the Norseman did not come south until three centuries later.

THE EARLY BISHOPS OF THE HOUSE OF STANLEY

But now I come to matters whereon I have more authority to speak. When the Isle of Man passed to the Stanley family, the Bishopric fell to their patronage, and they lost no time in putting their own people into it. It was then under the English metropolitan of Canterbury, but early in the sixteenth century it became part of the province of York. About that time the baronies, the abbeys, and the nunneries were suppressed. It does not appear that the change of metropolitan had made much change of religious life. Apparently the clergy kept the Manx people in miserable ignorance. It was not until the seventeenth century that the Book of Common Prayer was translated into the Manx language. The Gospels and the Acts were unknown to the Manx until nearly a century later. Nor was this due to ignorance of the clergy of the Manx tongue, for most of them must have been Manxmen, and several of the Bishops were Manxmen also. But grievous abuses had by this time attached themselves to the Manx Church, and some of them were flagrant and wicked, and some were impudent and amusing.

TITHES IN KIND

Naturally the more outrageous of the latter sort gathered about the process of collecting tithes. Tithes were paid in kind in those days. It was not until well within our own century that they were commuted to a money payment. The Manxman paid tithe on everything. He began to pay tithe before coming into the world, and he went on paying tithe even after he had gone out of it. This is a hard saying, but nevertheless a simple truth. Throughout his journey from the cradle to the grave, the Manxman paid tithe on all he inherited, on all he had, on all he did, on all his wife did, and on all he left behind him. We have the equivalent of this in England at the present hour, but it was yet more tyrannical, and infinitely more ludicrous, in the Isle of Man down to the year 1839. It is only vanity and folly and vexation of spirit to quarrel with the modern English tax gatherer; you are sure to go the wall, with humiliation and with disgrace. It was not always so when taxes were paid in kind. There was, at least, the satisfaction of cheating. The Manx people could not always deny themselves that satisfaction. For instance, they were required to pay tithe of herring as soon as the herring boats were brought above full sea mark, and there were ways of counting known to the fishermen with which the black-coated arithmeticians of the Church were not able to cope. A man paid tithe on such goods and even such clothes as his wife possessed on their wedding day, and young brides became wondrous wise in the selection for the vicarage of the garments that were out of fashion. A corpse-present was demanded over the grave of a dead man out of the horses and cattle whereof he died possessed, and dying men left verbal wills which consigned their broken-winded horses and dry cows to the mercy and care of the clergyman. You will not marvel much that such dealings led to disputes, sometimes to quarrels, occasionally to riots. In my boyhood I heard old people over the farm-house fire chuckle and tell of various wise doings, to outwit the parson. One of these concerned the oats harvest. When the oats were in sheaf, the parson's cart came up, driven by the sumner, the parson's official servant. The gate of the field was thrown open, and honestly and religiously one sheaf out of every ten was thrown into the cart. But the husbandman had been thrifty in advance. The parson's sheaves had all been grouped thick about the gate, and they were the shortest, and the thinnest, and the blackest, and the dirtiest, and the poorest that the field had yielded. Similar were the doings at the digging of the potatoes, but the scenes of recrimination which often ensued were usually confined to the farmer and the sumner. More outrageous contentions with the priest himself sometimes occurred within the very walls of the church. It was the practice to bring tithe of butter and cheese and eggs, and lay it on the altar on Sunday. This had to be done under pain of exclusion from the communion, and that was a penalty most grievous to material welfare. So the Manxmen and Manxwomen were compelled to go to church much as they went to market, with their butter- and egg- baskets over their arms. It is a ludicrous picture, as one sees it in one's mind's eye, but what comes after reaches the extremity of farce. Say the scene is Maughold old church, once the temple of the saintly hermit. It is Sunday morning, the bells are ringing, and Juan-beg-Marry-a-thruss, a rascally old skinflint, is coming along with a basket. It contains some butter that he could not sell at Ramsey market yesterday because it was rank, and a few eggs which he knows to be stale and addled—the old hen has sat on them, and they have brought forth nothing. These he places reverently on the altar. But the parson knows Juan, and proceeds to examine his tithe. May I take so much liberty with history, and with the desecrated old church, as to imagine the scene which follows?

Priest, pointing contemptuously towards the altar: "Juan-beg-Marry-a-thruss, what is this?"

"Butter and eggs, so plaze your reverence."

"Pig-swill and chalk you mean, man!"

"Aw 'deed if I'd known your reverence was so morthal partic'lar the ould hen herself should have been layin' some fresh eggs for your reverence."

"Take them away, you thief of the Church! Do you think what isn't fit for your pig is good enough for your priest? Bring better, or never let me look on your wizened old wicked face again."

Exit Juan-beg-Marry-a-thruss, perhaps with butter and eggs flying after his retreating figure.

THE GAMBLING BISHOP

This is an imaginary picture, but no less outrageous things happened whereof the records remain. A demoralised laity usually co-exists with a demoralised clergy, and there are some bad stories of the Bishops who preceded the Reformation. There is one story of a Bishop of that period, who was a gross drunkard and notorious gambler. He played with his clergy as long as they had anything to lose, and then he played with a deemster and lost five hundred pounds himself. Poor little island, that had two such men for its masters, the one its master in the things of this world, the other its master in the things of the world to come! If anything is needful to complete the picture of wretchedness in which the poor Manx people must have existed then, it is the knowledge of what manner of man a deemster was in those days, what his powers were, and how he exercised them.

THE DEEMSTERS

The two deemsters—a name of obvious significance, deemsters, such as deem the laws—were then the only judges of the island, all other legal functionaries being of more recent date. On entering into office, the deemster took an oath, which is sworn by all deemsters to this day, declaring by the wonderful works which God hath miraculously wrought in six days and seven nights, that he would execute the laws of the island justly "betwixt party and party, as indifferently as the herring's backbone doth lie in the midst of the fish." But these laws down to the time of the second Stanley existed only in the breasts of the deemsters themselves, being therefore called Breast Laws, and thus they were supposed to be handed down orally from deemster to deemster. The superstition fostered corruption as well as incapacity, and it will not be wronging the truth to say that some of the deemsters of old time were both ignorant and unprincipled. Their jurisdiction was absolute in all that were then thought to be temporal affairs, beginning with a debt of a shilling, and going up to murder. They kept their courts in the centres of their districts, one of them being in the north of the island, the other in the south, but they were free to hold a court anywhere, and at any time. A deemster riding from Ramsey to Peel might find his way stopped by a noisy claimant, who held his defendant by the lug, having dragged him bodily from the field to the highway, to receive instant judgment from the judge riding past. Or at midnight, in his own home, a deemster might be broken in upon by a clamorous gang of disputants and their witnesses, who came from the pot-house for the settlement of their differences. On such occasions, the deemster invariably acted on the sound old legal maxim, once recognised by an Act of Parliament, that suits not likely to bear good costs should always be settled out of court. First, the deemster demanded his fee. If neither claimant nor defendant could give it, he probably troubled himself no further than to take up his horse whip and drive both out into the road. I dare say there were many good men among deemsters of the old order, who loved justice for its own sake, and liked to see the poor and the weak righted, but the memory of deemsters of this kind is not green. The bulk of men are not better than their opportunities, and the temptations of the deemsters of old were neither few nor slight.

THE BISHOPRIC VACANT

With such masters in the State, and such masters in the Church, the island fell low in material welfare, and its poverty reacted on both. Within fifty years the Bishopric was nineteen years vacant, though it may be that at the beginning of the seventeenth century this was partly due to religious disturbances. Then in 1697, with the monasteries and nunneries dispersed, the abbeys in ruins, the cathedral church a wreck, the clergy sunk in sloth and ignorance, there came to the Bishopric, four years vacant, a true man whose name on the page of Manx Church history is like a star on a dark night, when only one is shining—Bishop Thomas Wilson. He was a strange and complex creature, half angel, only half man, the serenest of saints, and yet almost the bitterest of tyrants. Let me tell you about him.

BISHOP WILSON

Thomas Wilson was from Trinity College, Dublin, and became domestic chaplain to William, Earl of Derby, and preceptor to the Earl's son, who died young. While he held this position, the Bishopric of Sodor and Man became vacant, and it was offered to him. He declined it, thinking himself unworthy of so high a trust. The Bishopric continued vacant. Perhaps the candidates for it were few; certainly the emoluments were small; perhaps the patron was slothful—certainly he gave little attention to the Church. At length complaint was made to the King that the spiritual needs of the island were being neglected. The Earl was commanded to fill the Bishopric, and once again he offered it to his chaplain. Then Wilson yielded. He took possession in 1698, and was enthroned at Peel Castle. The picture of his enthronement must have been something to remember. Peel Castle was already tumbling to its fall, and the cathedral church was a woeful wreck. It is even said that from a hole in the roof the soil and rain could enter, and blades of grass were shooting up on the altar. The Bishop's house at Kirk Michael, which had been long shut up, was in a similar plight; damp, mouldy, broken-windowed, green with moss within and without. What would one give to turn back the centuries and look on at that primitive ceremony in St. Germain's Chapel in April 1698! There would be the clergy, a sorry troop, with wise and good men among them, no doubt, but a poor, battered, bedraggled, neglected lot, chiefly learned in dubious arts of collecting tithes. And the Bishop himself, the good chaplain of Earl Derby, the preceptor of his son, what a face he must have had to watch and to study, as he stood there that April morning, and saw for the first time what work he had come to tackle!

BISHOP WILSON'S CENSURES

But Bishop Wilson set about his task with a strong heart, and a resolute hand. He found himself in a twofold trust. Since the Reformation, the monasteries and nunneries had been dispersed, and all the baronies had been broken up, save one, the barony of the Bishop. Thus Bishop Wilson was the head of the court of his barony. This was a civil court with power of jurisdiction over felonies. Its separate criminal control came to an end in 1777. Such was Bishop Wilson's position as last and sole Baron of Man. Then as head of the Church he had powers over offences which were once called offences against common law. Irregular behaviour, cursing, quarrelling, and drinking, as well as transgressions of the moral code, adultery, seduction, prostitution, and the like, were punishable by the Church and the Church courts. The censures of Bishop Wilson on such offences did not err on the side of clemency. He was the enemy of sin, and no "gentle foe of sinners." He was a believer in witchcraft, and for suspicion of commerce with evil spirits and possession of the evil eye he punished many a blameless old body. For open and convicted adultery he caused the offenders to stand for an hour at high fair at each of the market-places of Douglas, Peel, Ramsey, and Castletown, bearing labels on their breasts calling on all people to take warning lest they came under the same Church censure. Common unchastity he punished by exposure in church at full congregation, when the guilty man or the poor victimised girl stepped up from the west porch to the altar, covered from neck to heels in a white sheet. Slanderers and evil speakers he clapped into the Peel, or perhaps the whipping-stocks, with tongue in a noose of leather, and when after a lapse of time the gag was removed the liberated tongue was obliged to denounce itself by saying thrice, clearly, boldly, probably with good accent and discretion, "False tongue, thou hast lied."

It is perhaps as well that some of us did not live in Bishop Wilson's time. We might not have lived long. If the Church still held and exercised the same powers over evil speakers we should never hear our own ears in the streets for the din of the voices of the penitents; and if it still punished unchastity in a white sheet the trade of the linen weaver would be brisk.

You will say that I have justified my statement that Bishop Wilson was the bitterest of tyrants. Let me now establish my opinion that he was also the serenest of saints. I have told you how low was the condition of the Church, how lax its rule, how deep its clergy lay in sloth and ignorance, and perhaps also in vice, when Bishop Wilson came to Man in 1698. Well, in 1703, only five years later, the Lord Chancellor King said this: "If the ancient discipline of the Church were lost elsewhere it might be found in all its force in the Isle of Man." This points first to force and vigour on the Bishop's part, but surely it also points to purity of character and nobility of aim. Bishop Wilson began by putting his own house in order. His clergy ceased to gamble and to drink, and they were obliged to collect their tithes with mercy. He once suspended a clergyman for an opinion on a minor point, but many times he punished his clergy for offences against the moral law and the material welfare of the poor. In a stiff fight for integrity of life and purity of thought, he spared none. I truly believe that if he had caught himself in an act of gross injustice he would have clambered up into the pillory. He was a brave, strong-hearted creature, of the build of a great man. Yes! In spite of all his contradictions, he *was* a great man. We Manxmen shall never look upon his like again!

THE GREAT CORN FAMINE

Towards 1740 a long and terrible corn famine fell upon our island. The fisheries had failed that season, and the crops had been blighted two years running. Miserably poor at all times, ill-clad, ill-housed, ill-fed at the best, the people were in danger of sheer destitution. In that day of their bitter trouble the poorest of the poor trooped off to Bishop's court. The Bishop threw open his house to them all, good and bad, improvident and thrifty, lazy and industrious, drunken and sober; he made no distinctions in that bad hour. He asked no man for his name who couldn't give it, no woman for her marriage lines who hadn't got them, no child whether it was born in wedlock. That they were all hungry was all he knew, and he saved their lives in thousands. He bought ship-loads of English corn and served it out in bushels; also tons of Irish potatoes, and served them out in *kischens*. He gave orders that the measure was to be piled as high as it would hold, and never smoothed flat again. Yet he was himself a poor man. While he had money he spent it. When every penny was gone he pledged his revenue in advance. After his credit was done he begged in England for his poor people in Man—*he* begged for *us* who would not have held out his hat to save his own life! God bless him! But we repaid him. Oh yes, we repaid him. His money he never got back, but gold is not the currency of the other world. Prayers and blessings are the wealth that is there, and these went up after him to the great White Throne from the swelling throats of his people.

THE BISHOP AT COURT

Not of Bishop Wilson could it be said, as it was said of another, that he "flattered princes in the temple of God." One day, when he was coming to Court, Queen Caroline saw him and said to a company of Bishops and Archbishops that surrounded her, "See, my lords, here is a Bishop who does not come for a translation." "No, indeed, and please your Majesty," said Bishop Wilson, "I will not leave my wife in her old age because she is poor." When Bishop Wilson was an old man. Cardinal Fleury sent over to ask after his age and health, saying that they were the two oldest and poorest Bishops in the world. At the same time he got an order that no French privateer should ever ravage the Isle of Man. The order has long lapsed, but I am told that to this day French seamen respect a Manxman. It touches me to think of it that thus does the glory of this good man's life shine on our faces still.

STORIES OF BISHOP WILSON

How his people must have loved him! Many of the stories told of him are of rather general application, but some of them ought to be true if they are not.

One day in the old three-cornered market-place at Ramsey a little maiden of seven crossed his path. She was like sunshine, rosy-cheeked, bright-eyed, bare-footed and bare-headed, and for love of her sweetness the grey old Bishop patted her head and blest her. "God bless you, my child; God bless you," he said. The child curtseyed and answered, "God bless you, too, sir." "Thank you, child, thank you," the Bishop said again; "I dare say your blessing will be as good as mine."

It was customary in those days, and indeed down to my

own time, when a suit of clothes was wanted, to have the journeyman tailor at home to make it. One, Danny of that ilk, was once at Bishop's Court making a long walking coat for the Bishop. In trying it on in its nebulous condition, that leprosy of open white seams and stitches, Danny made numerous chalk marks to indicate the places of the buttons. "No, no, Danny," said the Bishop, "no more buttons than enough to fasten it—only one, that will do. It would ill become a poor priest like me to go a-glitter with things like those." Now, Danny had already bought his buttons, and had them at that moment in his pocket. So, pulling a woeful face, he said, "Mercy me, my lord, what would happen to the poor button-makers, if everybody was of your opinion?" "Button it all over, Danny," said the Bishop. A coat of Bishop Wilson's still exists. Would that we had that one of the numerous buttons, and could get a few more made of the same pattern! It would be out of fashion—Danny's progeny have taken care of that. There are not many of us that it would fit—we have few men of Bishop Wilson's build nowadays. But human kindliness is never old-fashioned, and there are none of us that the garment of sweet grace would not suit.

QUARRELS OF CHURCH AND STATE

So far from "flattering princes in the temple of God," Bishop Wilson was even morbidly jealous of the authority of the Church, and he resisted that of the State when the civil powers seemed to encroach upon it. More than once he came into collision with the State's highest functionary, the Lieutenant-Governor, representative of the Lord of Man himself. One day the Governor's wife falsely defamed a lady, and the lady appealed to the Bishop. Thereupon the Bishop interdicted the Governor's wife from receiving the communion. But the Governor's chaplain admitted her. Straightaway the Bishop suspended the Governor's chaplain. Then the Governor fined the Bishop in the sum of fifty pounds. The Bishop refused to pay, and was committed to Castle Rushen, and lay there two months. They show us his cell, a poor, dingy little box, so damp in his day that he lost the use of some of his fingers. After that the Bishop appealed to the Lord, who declared the imprisonment illegal. The Bishop was liberated, and half the island went to the prison gate to fetch him forth in triumph. The only result was that the Bishop lost £500, whereof £300 were subscribed by the people. One hardly knows whether to laugh or cry at it all. It is a sorry and silly farce. Of course it made a tremendous hurly-burly in its day, but it is gone now, and doesn't matter a ha'porth to anybody. Nevertheless because Gessler's cap goes up so often nowadays, and so many of us are kneeling to it, it is good and wholesome to hear of a poor Bishop who was brave enough to take a shot at it instead.

SOME OLD ORDEALS

Notwithstanding Bishop Wilson's severity, his tyranny, his undue pride in the authority of the Church, and his morbid jealousy of the powers of the State, his rule was a wise and just one, and he was a spiritual statesman, who needed not to be ashamed. He raised the tone of life in the Isle of Man, made it possible to accept a man's *yea* and *nay*, even in those perilous issues of life where the weakness and meanness of poor humanity reveals itself in lies and subterfuges. This he did by making false swearing a terror. One ancient ordeal of swearing he set his face against, but another he encouraged, and often practised. Let me describe both.

In the old days, when a man died intestate, leaving no

record of his debts, a creditor might establish a claim by going with the Bishop to the grave of the dead man at midnight, stretching himself on it with face towards heaven and a Bible on his breast, and then saying solemnly, "I swear that So-and-so, who lies buried here, died in my debt by so much." After that the debt was allowed. What warning the Bishop first pronounced I do not know, but the scene is a vivid one, even if we think of the creditor as swearing truly, and a startling and terrible one if we think of him as about to swear to what is false. The dark night, the dark figures moving in it, the churchyard, the debtor's grave, the sham creditor, who had been loud in his protests under the light of the inn of the village, now quaking and trembling as the Bishop's warning comes out of the gloom, then stammering, and breaking down, and finally, with ghostly visions of a dead hand clutching at him from the grave, starting up, shrieking, and flying away. It is a nightmare. Let us not remember it when the candles are put out.

This ordeal was in force until the seventeenth century, but Bishop Wilson judged it un-Christian, and never practised it. The old Roman canon law of Purgation, a similar ordeal, he used not rarely. It was designed to meet cases of slander in which there was no direct and positive evidence. If a good woman had been accused of unchastity in that vague way of rumour which is always more damaging and devilish than open accusation, she might of her own free choice, or by compulsion of the Bishop, put to silence her false accusers by appearing in church, with witnesses ready to take oath that they believed her, and there swearing at the altar that common fame and suspicion had wronged her. If a man doubted her word he had to challenge it, or keep silence for ever after. The severest censures of the Church were passed upon those who dared to repeat an unproved accusation after the oaths of Purgation and Compurgation had been taken unchallenged. It is a fine, honest ordeal, very old, good for the right, only bad for the wrong, giving strength to the weak and humbling the mighty. But it would be folly and mummery in our day. The Church has lost its powers over life and limb, and no one capable of defaming a pure woman would care a brass penny about the Church's ex-communication. Yet a woman's good name is the silver thread that runs through the pearl chain of her virtues. Pity that nowadays it can be so easily snapped. Conversation at five o'clock tea is enough to do that. The ordeal of compulsory Purgation was abolished in Man as late as 1737.

THE HERRING FISHERY

Bishop Wilson began, or revived, a form of service which was so beautiful, so picturesque, and withal so Manx that I regret the loss of scarce any custom so much as the discontinuance of this one. It was the fishermen's service on the shore at the beginning of the herring-season. But in order to appreciate it you must first know something of the herring fishing itself. It is the chief industry of the island. Half the population is connected with it in some way. A great proportion of the men of the humbler classes are half seamen, half landsmen, tilling their little crofts in the spring and autumn, and going out with the herring boats in summer. The herring is the national fish. The Manxman swears by its flavour. The deemsters, as we have seen, literally swear by its backbone. Potatoes and herrings constitute a common dish of the country people. They are ready for it at any hour of the day or night. I have had it for dinner, I have taken it for supper, I have seen it for tea, and even known it for breakfast. It is served without ceremony. In the middle of the table two great crocks, one of potatoes boiled in their jackets, the other of herrings fresh or salted; a plate and a bowl of new milk at every seat, and lumps of salt here and there. To be a Manxman you must eat Manx herrings; there is a story that to transform himself into a Manxman one of the Dukes of Athol ate twenty-four of them at breakfast, a herring for every member of his House of Keys.

The Manx herring fishery is interesting and very picturesque. You know that the herrings come from northern latitudes. Towards mid-winter a vast colony of them set out from the arctic seas, closely pursued by innumerable sea-fowl, which deal death among the little emigrants. They move in two divisions, one westward towards the coasts of America, the other eastward in the direction of Europe. They reach the Shetlands in April and the Isle of Man about June. The herring is fished at night. To be out with the herring boats is a glorious experience on a calm night. You have set sail with the fleet of herring boats about sun-down, and you are running before a light breeze through the dusk. The sea-gulls are skimming about the brown sails of your boat. They know what you are going to do, and have come to help you. Presently you come upon a flight of them wheeling and diving in the gathering darkness. Then you know that you have lit on the herring shoal. The boat is brought head to the wind and left to drift. By this time the stars are out, perhaps the moon also—though too much moon is not good for the fishing—and you can just descry the dim outline of the land against the dark blue of the sky. Luminous patches of phosphorescent light begin to move in the water. "The mar-fire's rising," say the fishermen, the herring are stirring. "Let's make a shot; up with the gear," cries the skipper, and nets are hauled from below, passed over the bank-board, and paid out into the sea—a solid wall of meshes, floating upright, nine feet deep and a quarter of a mile long. It is a calm, clear night, just light enough to see the buoys on the back of the first net. The lamp is fixed on the mitch-board. All is silence, only the steady plash, plash, plash of the slow waters on the boat's side; no singing among the men, no chaff, no laughter, all quiet aboard, for the fishermen believe that the fish can hear; all quiet around, where the deep black of the watery pavement is brightened by the reflection of stars. Then out of the white phosphorescent patches come minute points of silver and countless faint popping sounds. The herrings are at play about the nets. You see them in numbers exceeding imagination, shoals on shoals. "Pull up now, there's a heavy strike," cries the skipper, and the nets are hauled up, and come in white and moving—a solid block of fish, cheep, cheep, cheeping like birds in the early morning. At the grey of dawn the boats begin to run for home, and the sun is shining as the fleet makes the harbour. Men and women are waiting there to buy the night's catch. The quay is full of them, bustling, shouting, laughing, quarrelling, counting the herrings, and so forth.

THE FISHERMEN'S SERVICE

Such is the herring fishery of Man. Bishop Wilson knew how bitter a thing it could be if this industry failed the island even for a single season. So, with absolute belief in the Divine government of the world, he wrote a Service to be held on the first day of the herring season, asking for God's blessing on the harvest of the sea. The scene of that service must have been wondrously beautiful and impressive. Why does not some great painter paint it? Let me, by the less, effectual vehicle of words, attempt to realise what it must have been.

The place of it was Peel bay, a wide stretch of beach, with a gentle slope to the left, dotted over with grey houses; the little town farther on, with its nooks and corners, its blind alleys and dark lanes, its narrow, crabbed, crooked streets. Behind this the old pier and the herring boats rocking in the harbour, with their brown sails half set, waiting for the top of the tide. In the distance the broad breast of Contrary Head, and, a musket-shot outside of it, the little rocky islet whereon stand the stately ruins of the noble old Peel Castle. The beach is dotted over with people—old men, in their curranes and undyed stockings, leaning on their sticks; children playing on the shingle; young women in groups, dressed in sickle-shaped white sun-bonnets, and with petticoats tucked up; old women in long blue homespun cloaks. But these are only the background of the human picture. In the centre of it is a wide circle of fishermen, men and boys, of all sizes and sorts, from the old Admiral of the herring fleet to the lad that helps the cook—rude figures in blue and with great sea-boots. They are on their knees on the sand, with their knitted caps at their rusty faces, and in the middle of them, standing in an old broken boat, is the Bishop himself, bare-headed, white-headed, with upturned face praying for the fishing season that is about to begin. The June day is sweet and beautiful, and the sun is going down behind the castle. Some sea-gulls are disporting on the rock outside, and, save for their jabbering cries, and the boom of the sea from the red horizon, and the gentle plash of the wavelets on the pebbles of the shore, nothing is heard but the slow tones of the Bishop and the fishermen's deep Amen. Such was Bishop Wilson's fishermen's service. It is gone; more's the pity.

SOME OLD LAWS

The spiritual laws of Man were no dead letters when Bishop Wilson presided over its spiritual courts. He was good to illegitimate children, making them legitimate if their parents married within two years of their birth, and often putting them on the same level with their less injured brothers and sisters where inheritance was in question. But he was unmerciful to the parents themselves. There is one story of his treatment of a woman which passes all others in its tyranny. It is, perhaps, the only deep stain on his character. I thank God that it can never have come to the ears of Victor Hugo. Told as Hugo would have told it, surely it must have blasted for ever the name of a good man. It is the dark story of Katherine Kinrade.

KATHERINE KINRADE

She was a poor ruin of a woman, belonging to Kirk Christ, but wandering like a vagrant over the island. The fact of first consequence is, that she was only half sane. In the language of the clergy of the time, she "had a degree of unsettledness and defect of understanding." Thus she was the sort of human wreck that the world finds it easy to fling away. Katherine fell victim to the sin that was not her own. A child was born. The Church censured her. She did penance in a white sheet at the church doors. But her poor, dull brain had no power to restrain her. A second child was born. Then the Bishop committed her for twenty-one days to his prison at the Peel. Let me tell you what the place is like. It is a crypt of the cathedral church. You enter it by a little door in the choir, leading to a tortuous flight of steep steps going down. It is a chamber cut out of the rock of the little island, dark, damp, and noisome. A small aperture lets in the light, as well as the sound of the sea beating on the rocks below. The roof, if you could see it in the gloom, is groined and ribbed, and above it is the mould of many graves, for in the old days bodies were buried in the choir. Can you imagine a prison more terrible for any prisoner, the strongest man or the bravest soldier? Think of it on a tempestuous night in winter. The lonely islet rock, with the swift seas rushing around it; the castle half a ruin, its guard-room empty, its banqueting hall roofless, its sally port silent; then the cathedral church falling to decay; and under the floor of its choir, where lie the graves of dead men, this black, grim, cold cell, silent as the graves themselves, save for the roar of the sea as it beats in the darkness on the rocks outside! But that is not enough. We have to think of this gloomy pile as inhabited on such a night of terrors by only one human soul—this poor, bedraggled, sin-laden woman with "the defect of understanding." Can anything be more awful? Yet there is worse to follow. The records tell us that Katherine Kinrade submitted to her punishment "with as much discretion as could be expected of the like of her." But such punishments do not cleanse the soul that is "drenched with unhallowed fire." Perhaps Katherine did not know that she was wronged; nevertheless God's image was being trodden out of her. She went from bad to worse, became a notorious strumpet, strolled about the island, and led "a scandalous life on other accounts." A third child was born. Then the Bishop concluded that for the honour of the Christian name, "to prevent her own utter destruction, and for the example of others," a timely and thorough reformation must be made by a further and severer punishment. It was the 15th day of March, and he ordered that on the 17th day, being the fair of St. Patrick, at the height of the market, the said Katherine Kinrade should be taken to Peel Town in charge of the general sumner, and the constables and soldiers of the garrison, and there dragged after a boat in the sea! Think of it! On a bitter day in March this wretched woman with the "defect of understanding" was to be dragged through the sea by a rope tied to the tail of a boat! And if any owner, master, and crew of any boat proved refractory by refusing to perform this service for the restraining of vice, they were to be subject to fine and imprisonment! When St.

Patrick's Day came the weather was so stormy that no boat could live in the bay, but on St. Germain's Day, about the height of the market, the censure was performed. After undergoing the punishment the miserable soul was apparently penitent, "according to her capacity," took the communion, and was "received into the peace of the Church." Poor human ruin, defaced image of a woman, begrimed and buried soul, unchaste, mis-shapen, incorrigible, no "juice of God's distilling" ever "dropped into the core of her life," to such punishment she was doomed by the tribunal of that saintly man, Bishop Thomas Wilson! She has met him at another tribunal since then; not where she has crouched before him, but where she has stood by his side. She has carried her great account against him, to Him before whom the proudest are as chaff.

None spake when Wilson stood before
     The Throne;
     And He that sat thereon
Spake not; and all the presence-floor
Burnt deep with blushes, and the angels cast
Their faces downwards.—Then, at last,
     Awe-stricken, he was ware
     How on the emerald stair
A woman sat divinely clothed in white,
And at her knees four cherubs bright,
     That laid
Their heads within her lap. Then, trembling, he essayed
     To speak—"Christ's mother, pity me!"
Then answered she,
"Sir, I am Katherine Kinrade."*

* Unpublished poem by the author of "Fo'c'sle Yarns."

BISHOP WILSON'S LAST DAYS

Have I dashed your faith in my hero? Was he indeed the bitterest of tyrants as well as the serenest of saints? Yet bethink you of the other good men who have done evil deeds? King David and the wife of Uriah, Mahomet and his adopted son; the gallery of memory is hung round with many such portraits. Poor humanity, weak at the strongest, impure at the purest; best take it as it is, and be content. Remember that a good man's vices are generally the excess of his virtues. It was so with Bishop Wilson. Remember, too, that it is not for what a man does, but for what he means to do, that we love him or hate him in the end. And in the end the Manx people loved Bishop Wilson, and still they bless his memory.

We have a glimpse of his last days, and it is full of tender beauty. True to his lights, simple and frugal of life. God-fearing and strong of heart, he lived to be old. Very feeble, his beautiful face grown mellower even as his heart was softer for his many years, tottering on his staff, drooping like a white flower, he went in and out among his people, laying his trembling hands on the children's heads and blessing them, remembering their fathers and their fathers' fathers. Beloved by the young, reverenced by the old, honoured by the great, worshipped by the poor, living in sweet patience, ready to die in hope. His day was done, his night was near, and the weary toiler was willing to go to his rest. Thus passed some peaceful years. He died in 1755, and was followed to his grave by the whole Manx nation. His tomb is our most sacred shrine. We know his faults, but we do not speak of them there. Call a truce over the place of the old man's rest. There he lies, who was once the saviour of our people. God bless him! He was our fathers' bishop, and his saintly face still shines on our fathers' children.

THE ATHOL BISHOPS

Let me in a last clause attempt a sketch of the history of the Manx Church in the century or more that has followed Bishop Wilson's death. The last fifty years of it are featureless, save for an attempt to abolish the Bishopric. This foolish effort first succeeded and then failed, and was a poor bit of mummery altogether, ending in nothing but waste of money and time, and breath and temper. The fifty years immediately succeeding Bishop Wilson were full of activity. But so far as the Church was concerned, the activity was not always wholesome. If religion was kept alive in Man in those evil days, and the soul hunger of the poor Manx people was satisfied, it was not by the masters of the Manx Church, the Pharisees who gave alms in the streets to the sound of a trumpet going before them, or by the Levites who passed by on the other side when a man had fallen among thieves. It was partly by dissent, which was begun by Wesley in 1775 (after Quakerism had been suppressed), and partly by a small minority of the Manx clergy, who kept going the early evangelicalism of Newton and Cowper and Cecil—dear, sunny, simple-hearted old Manx vicars, who took sweet counsel together in their old-fashioned homes, where you found grace in all senses of the word, purity of soul, the life of the mind, and gentle courtliness of manners.

Bishop Wilson's successor was Doctor Mark Hildlesley, in all respects a worthy man. He completed the translation of the Scriptures into Manx, which had been begun by his predecessor, and established Sunday-schools in Man before they had been commenced in any other country. But after him came a line of worthless prelates, Dr. Richmond, remembered for his unbending haughtiness; Dr. Mason, disgraced by his debts; and Claudius Cregan, a bishop unfit to be a curate. Do you not read between the broad lines of such facts? The Athol dynasty was now some thirty years established in Man, and the swashbuckler Court of fine gentlemen was in full swing. In that costume drama of soiled lace and uproarious pleasures, what part did the Church play? Was it that of the man clad in camel's skin, living on locusts and wild honey, and calling on the generation of revellers to flee from the wrath to come? No; but that of the lover of cakes and ale. The records of this period are few and scanty, but they are full enough to show that some of the clergy of the Athols knew more of backgammon than of theology. While they pandered to the dissolute Court they lived under, going the errands of their masters in the State, fetching and carrying for them, and licking their shoes, they tyrannised over the poor ignorant Manx people and fleeced them unmercifully. Perhaps this was in a way only natural. Corruption was in the air throughout Europe. Dr. Youngs were grovelling for preferments at the feet of kings' mistresses, and Dr. Warners were kissing the shoebuckles of great ladies for sheer love of their faces, plastered red and white. The parasites of the Manx clergy were not far behind some of their English brethren. There is a story told of their life among themselves which casts lurid light on their character and ways of life. It is said that two of the Vicars-general summoned a large number of the Manx people to Bishop's Court on some business of the spiritual court. Many of the people had come long distances, chiefly a-foot, without food, and probably without money. After a short sitting the court was adjourned for dinner. The people had no dinner, and they starved. The Vicars-general went into the palace to dine with the Bishop. Some hours passed. The night was gathering. Then a message came out to say that no more business could be done that day. Some of the poor people were old, and had to travel fifteen miles to their homes. The record tells us that the Bishop gave his guests "most excellent wine." What of a scene like that? Outside, a sharp day in Spring, two score famished folks tramping the glen and the gravel-path, the gravel-path and the glen, to and fro, to and fro, minute after minute, hour after hour. Inside, my lord Bishop, drenched in debt, dining with his clergy, drinking "most excellent wine" with them, unbending his mighty mind with them, exchanging boisterous stories with them, jesting with them, laughing with them, until his face grows as red as the glowing turf on his hearth. Presently a footfall on the gravel, and outside the window a hungry, pinched, anxious face looking nervously into the room. Then this colloquy:

"Ah, the court, plague on't, I'd forgotten it."

"Adjourn it, gentlemen."

"Wine like yours, my lord, would make a man forget Paradise."

"Sit down again, gentlemen. Juan, go out and tell the people to come back to-morrow."

"Your right good health, my lord!"

"And yours, gentlemen both!"

Oh, if there is any truth in religion, if this world is God's, if a day is coming when the weak shall be exalted and the mighty laid low, what a reckoning they have gone to whose people cried for bread and they gave them a stone! And if there is not, if the hope is vain, if it is all a sham and a mockery, still the justice of this world is sure. Where are they now, these parasites? Their game is played out. They are bones and ashes; they are in their forgotten graves.

THE STORY OF THE MANX PEOPLE

THE MANX LANGUAGE

A FRIEND asked me the other day if there was any reason why I should not deliver these lectures in Manx. I answered that there were just forty good and sufficient reasons. The first was that I did not speak Manx. Like the wise queen in the story of the bells, he then spared me the recital of the remaining nine-and-thirty. But there is at least one of the number that will appeal strongly to most of my hearers. What that is you shall judge for yourselves after I have braved the pitfalls of pronunciation in a tongue I do not know, and given you some clauses of the Lord's Prayer in Manx.

> *Ayr ain fayms niau,*
> (Father our who art in heaven.)
> *Caskerick dy row dty ennym,*
> (Holy be Thy name.)
> *Dy jig dty reeriaght,*
> (Come Thy kingdom.)
> *Dty aigney dy row jeant er y thalloo mry te ayns niau,*
> (Thy will be done on the earth even as in heaven.)
> *Son dy bragh, as dy bragh, Amen.*
> (For ever and ever. Amen.)

I asked a friend—it was Mr. Wilson Barrett—if in its fullness, its fine chest-notes, its force and music, this old language did not sound like Italian.

"Well, no," he answered, "it sounds more like hard swearing."

I think you must now understand why the greater part of these lectures should be delivered in English.

Manx is a dialect mainly Celtic, and differing only slightly from the ancient Scottish Gaelic. I have heard my father say that when he was a boy in Ramsey, sixty years ago, a Scotch ship came ashore on the Canick, and next morning after the wreck a long, lank, bony creature, with bare legs, and in short petticoats, came into the marketplace and played a tune on a little shrieking pair of smithy bellows, and then sang a song. It was a Highland piper, and he sang in his Gaelic, but the Manx boys and girls who gathered round him understood almost every word of his song, though they thought his pronunciation bad. Perhaps they took him for a poor old Manxman, somehow strayed and lost, a sort of Manx Rip Van Winkle who had slept a century in Scotland, and thereby lost part of his clothes.

You will wonder that there is not more Norse in our language, remembering how much of the Norse is in our blood. But the predominance of the Celtic is quite natural. Our mothers were Celts, speaking Celtic, before our Norse fathers came. Was it likely that our Celtic mothers should learn much of the tongue of their Norse husbands? Then, is it not our mother, rather than our father, who teaches us to speak when we are children? So our Celtic mothers taught us Celtic, and thus Celtic became the dominant language of our race.

MANX NAMES

But though our Norse fathers could not impose their Norse tongue on their children, they gave them Norse names, and to the island they gave Norse place-names. Hence we find that though Manx names show a preponderance of the Celtic, yet that the Norse are numerous and important. Thus we have many *dales*, *fells*, *garths*, and *ghylls*. Indeed, we have many pure Scandinavian surnames and place-names. When I was in Iceland I sometimes found myself face to face with names which almost persuaded me that I was at home in our little island of the Irish Sea. There is, for example, a Snaefell in Man as well as in Iceland. Then, our Norwegian surnames often took Celtic prefixes, such as Mac, and thus became Scandio-Gaelic. But this is a subject on which I have no right to speak with authority. You will find it written down with learning and judgment in the good book of my friend Mr. A. W. Moore, of Cronkbourne. What concerns me more than the scientific aspect of the language is its literary character. I seem to realise that it was the language of a poetic race. The early generations of a people are often poetic. They are child-like, and to be like a child is the best half of being like a poet. They name their places by help of their observatory powers. These are fresh and full of wonder, and Nature herself is beautiful or strange until man tampers with her. So when an untaught and uncorrupted mind looks upon a new scene and bethinks itself of a name to fit it, the name is almost certainly full of charm or rugged power. Thus we find in Man such mixed Norse and Celtic names as: *Booildooholly* (Black fold of the wood), *Douglas* (Black stream), *Soderick* (South creek), *Trollaby* (Troll's farm), *Gansy* (Magic isle), *Cronk-y-Clagh Bane* (Hill of the white stone), *Cronk-ny-hey* (Hill of the grave), *Cronk-ny-arrey-lhaa* (Hill of the day watch).

MANX IMAGINATION

This poetic character of the place-names of the island is a standing reproach to us as a race. We have degenerated in poetic spirit since such names were the natural expression of our feelings. I tremble to think what our place-names would be if we had to make them now. Our few modern christenings set my teeth on edge. We are not a race of poets. We are the prosiest of the prosy. I have never in my life met

with any race, except Icelanders and Norwegians, who are
so completely the slave of hard fact. It is astounding how
difficult the average Manxman finds it to put himself into the
mood of the poet. That anything could come out of nothing,
that there is such a thing as imagination, that any human
brother of an honest man could say that a thing had been,
which had not been, and yet not lie—these are bewildering
difficulties to the modern Manxman. That a novel can be
false and yet true—that, well that's foolishness. I wrote a
Manx romance called "The Deemster;" and I did not expect
my fellow-countrymen of the primitive kind to tolerate it for
a moment. It was merely a fiction, and the true Manxman of
the old sort only believes in what is true. He does not read
very much, and when he does read it is not novels. But he
could not keep his hands off this novel, and on the whole,
and in the long run, he liked it—that is, as he would say,
"middling," you know! But there was only one condition on
which he could take it to his bosom—it must be true. There
was the rub, for clearly it transgressed certain poor little facts
that were patent to everybody. Never mind. Hall Caine did
not know poor Man, or somebody had told him wrong. But
the story itself! The Bishop, Dan, Ewan, Mona, the body
coming ashore at the Mooragh, the poor boy Under the
curse by the Calf, lord-a-massy, that was thrue as gospel!
What do you think happened? I have got the letters by me,
and can show them to anybody. A good Manxman wrote to
remonstrate with me for calling the book a "romance." How
dare I do so? It was all true. Another wrote saying that maybe
I would like to know that in his youth he knew my poor hero,
Dan Mylrea, well. They often drank together. In fact, they
were the same as brothers. For his part he had often warned
poor Dan the way he was going. After the murder, Dan came
to him and gave him the knife with which he had killed
Ewan. He had got it still!

Later than the "Deemster," I published another Manx romance, "The Bondman." In that book I mentioned, without thought of mischief, certain names that must have been lying at the back of my head since my boyhood. One of them becomes in the book the name of an old hypocrite who in the end cheats everybody and yet prays loudly in public. Now it seems that there is a man up in the mountains who owns that name. When he first encountered it in the newspapers, where the story was being published as a serial, he went about saying he was in the "Bondman," that it was all thrue as gospel, so it was, that he knew me when I was a boy, over Ramsey way, and used to give me rides on his donkey, so he did. This was before the hypocrite was unmasked; and when that catastrophe occurred, and his villany stood naked before all the island, his anger knew no limits. I am told that he goes about the mountains now like a thunder-cloud, and that he wants to meet me. I had never heard of the man before in all my life.

What I say is true only of the typical Manxman, the natural-man among Manxmen, not of the Manxman who is Manxman plus man of the world, the educated Manxman, who finds it as easy as anybody else to put himself into a position of sympathy with works of pure imagination. But you must go down to the turf if you want the true smell of the earth. Education levels all human types, as love is said to level all ranks; and to preserve your individuality and yet be educated seems to want a strain of genius, or else a touch of madness.

The Manx must have been the language of a people with few thoughts to express, but such thoughts as they had were beautiful in their simplicity and charm, sometimes wise and shrewd, and not rarely full of feeling. Thus *laa-noo* is old Manx for child, and it means literally half saint—a sweet conception, which says the best of all that is contained in

Wordsworth's wondrous "Ode on the Intimations of Immortality." *Laa-bee* is old Manx for bed, literally half-meat, a profound commentary on the value of rest. The old salutation at the door of a Manx cottage before the visitor entered was this word spoken from the porch: *Vel peccaghs' thie?* Literally: Any sinner within? All humanity being sinners in the common speech of the Manx people.

MANX PROVERBS

Nearly akin to the language of a race are its proverbs, and some of the Manx proverbs are wise, witty, and racy of the soil. Many of them are the common possession of all peoples. Of such kind is "There's many a slip 'twixt the cup and the lip." Here is one which sounds like an Eastern saying: "Learning is fine clothes for the rich man, and riches for the poor man." But I know of no foreign parentage for a proverb like this: "A green hill when far away; bare, bare when it is near." That may be Eastern also. It hints of a long weary desert; no grass, no water, and then the cruel mirage that breaks down the heart of the wayfarer at last. On the other hand, it is not out of harmony with the landscape of Man, where the mountains look green sometimes from a distance when they are really bare and stark, and so typify that waste of heart when life is dry of the moisture of hope, and all the world is as a parched wilderness. However, there is one proverb which is so Manx in spirit that I could almost take oath on its paternity, so exactly does it fit the religious temper of our people, though it contains a word that must strike an English ear as irreverent: "When one poor man helps another poor man, God himself laughs."

MANX BALLADS

Next to the proverbs of a race its songs are the best expression of its spirit, and though Manx songs are few, some ot them are full of Manx character. Always their best part is the air. A man called Barrow compiled the Manx tunes about the beginning of the century, but his book is scarce. In my ignorance of musical science I can only tell you how the little that is left of Manx music lives in the ear of a man who does not know one note from another. Much of it is like a wail of the wind in a lonely place near to the sea, sometimes like the soughing of the long grass, sometimes like the rain whipping the panes of a window as with rods. Nearly always long-drawn like a moan, rarely various, never martial, never inspiriting, often sad and plaintive, as of a people kept under, but loving liberty, poor and low down, but with souls alive, looking for something, and hoping on,—full of the brine, the salt foam, the sad story of the sea. Nothing would give you a more vivid sense of the Manx people than some of our old airs. They would seem to take you into a little whitewashed cottage with sooty rafters and earthen floor, where an old man who looks half like a sailor and half like a landsman is dozing before a peat fire that is slumbering out. Have I in my musical benightedness conveyed an idea of anything musical? If not, let me, by the only vehicle natural to me, give you the rough-shod words of one or two of our old ballads. There is a ballad, much in favour, called *Ny kirree fo niaghtey*, the Sheep under the Snow. Another, yet better known, is called *Myle Charaine*. This has sometimes been called the Manx National Air, but that is a fiction. The song has nothing to do with the Manx as a nation. Perhaps it is merely a story of a miser and his daughter's dowry. Or perhaps it tells of pillage, probably of wrecking, basely done, and of how the people cut the guilty one off from all intercourse with them.

O, Myle Charaine, where got you your gold?
    Lone, lone, yon have left me here.
O, not in the curragh, deep under the mould,
    Lone, lone, and void of cheer.

This sounds poor enough, but it would be hard to say how deeply this ballad, wedded to its wailing music, touches and moves a Manxman. Even to my ear as I have heard it in Manx, it has seemed to be one of the weirdest things in old ballad literature, only to be matched by some of the old Irish songs, and by the gruesome ditty which tells how "the sun shines fair on Carlisle wa'."

MANX CAROLS

The paraphrase I have given you was done by George Borrow, who once visited the island. My friend the Rev. T. E. Brown met him and showed him several collections of Manx carols, and he pronounced them all translations from the English, not excepting our famous *Drogh Vraane*, or carol of every bad woman whose story is told in the Bible, beginning with the story of mother Eve herself. And, indeed, you will not be surprised that to the shores of our little island have drifted all kinds of miscellaneous rubbish, and that the Manxmen, from their very simplicity and ignorance of other literatures, have had no means of sifting the flotsam and assigning value to the constituents. Besides this, they are so irresponsible, have no literary conscience, and accordingly have appropriated anything and everything. This is true of some Manx ballads, and perhaps also of many Manx carols. The carols, called Carvals in Manx, serve in Man, as in other countries, the purpose of celebrating the birth of Jesus, but we have one ancient custom attached to them which we can certainly claim for our own, so Manx is it, so quaint, so grimly serious, and withal so howlingly ludicrous.

It is called the service of Oiel Verree, probably a corruption of *Feaill Vorrey*, literally the Feast of Mary, and it is held in the parish church near to midnight on Christmas Eve. Scott describes it in "Peveril of the Peak," but without personal knowledge.

Services are still held in many churches on Christmas Eve; and I think they are called Oiel Verree, but the true Oiel Verree, the real, pure, savage, ridiculous, sacrilegious old Oiel Verree, is gone. I myself just came in time for it; I saw the last of it, nevertheless I saw it at its prime, for I saw it when it was so strong that it could not live any longer. Let me tell you what it was.

The story carries me back to early boyish years, when, from the lonely school-house on the bleak top of Maughold Head, I was taken in secret, one Christmas Eve, between nine and ten o'clock, to the old church of Kirk Maughold, a parish which longer than any other upheld the rougher traditions. My companion was what is called an original. His name was Billy Corkill. We were great chums. I would be thirteen, he was about sixty. Billy lived alone in a little cottage on the high-road, and worked in the fields. He had only one coat all the years I knew him. It seemed to have been blue to begin with, but when it had got torn Billy had patched it with anything that was handy, from green cloth to red flannel. He called it his Joseph's coat of many colours. Billy was a poet and a musical composer. He could not read a word, but he would rather have died than confess his ignorance. He kept books and newspapers always about him, and when he read out of them, he usually held them upside down. If any one remarked on that, he said he could read them any way up— that was where his scholarship came in. Billy was a great carol singer. He did not know a note, but he never sang except from music. His tunes were wild harmonies that no human ear ever heard before. It will be clear to you that old Billy was a man of genius.

Such was my comrade on that Christmas Eve long ago. It had been a bitter winter in the Isle of Man, and the ground was covered with snow But the church bells rang merrily over the dark moorland, for Oiel Verree was peculiarly the people's service, and the ringers were ringing in the one service of the year at which the parishioners supplanted the Vicar, and appropriated the old parish church. In spite of the weather, the church was crowded with a motley throng, chiefly of young folks, the young men being in the nave, and the girls (if I remember rightly) in the little loft at the west end. Most of the men carried tallow dips, tied about with bits of ribbon in the shape of rosettes, duly lighted, and guttering grease at intervals on to the book-ledge or the tawny fingers of them that held them. It appeared that there had been an ordinary service before we arrived, and the Vicar was still within the rails of the communion. From there he addressed some parting words of solemn warning to the noisy throng of candle-carriers. As nearly as I can remember, the address was this: "My good people, you are about to celebrate an old custom. For my part, I have no sympathy with such customs, but since the hearts of my parishioners seem to be set on this one, I have no wish to suppress it. But tumultuous and disgraceful scenes have occurred on similar occasions in previous years, and I beg you to remember that you are in God's house," &c. &c. The grave injunction was listened to in silence, and when it ended, the Vicar, a worthy but not very popular man, walked towards the vestry. To do so, he passed the pew where I sat under the left arm of my companion, and he stopped before him, for Billy had long been a notorious transgressor at Oiel Verree.

"See that you do not disgrace my church to-night," said

the Vicar. But Billy had a biting tongue.

"Aw, well," said he, "I'm thinking the church is the people's."

"The people are as ignorant as goats," said the Vicar.

"Aw, then," said Billy, "you are the shepherd, so just make sheeps of them."

At that the Vicar gave us the light of his countenance no more. The last glimpse of his robe going through the vestry door was the signal for a buzz of low gossip, and straightway the business of Oiel Verree began.

It must have been now approaching eleven o'clock, and two old greybeards with tousled heads placed themselves abreast at the door of the west porch. There they struck up a carol in a somewhat lofty key. It was a most doleful ditty. Certainly I have never since heard the like of it. I remember that it told the story of the Crucifixion in startling language, full of realism that must have been horribly ghastly, if it had not been so comic. At the end of each verse the singers made one stride towards the communion. There were some thirty verses, and every mortal verse did these zealous carollers give us. They came to an end at length, and then another old fellow rose in his pew and sang a ditty in Manx. It told of the loss of the herring-fleet in Douglas Bay in the last century. After that there was yet another and another carol—some that might be called sacred, others that would not be badly wronged with the name of profane. As I recall them now, they were full of a burning earnestness, and pictured the dangers of the sinner and the punishment of the damned. They said nothing about the joys of heaven, or the pleasures of life. Wherever these old songs came from they must have dated from some period of religious revival. The Manxman may have appropriated them, but if he did so he was in a deadly earnest mood. It must have been like stealing a hat-band.

My comrade had been silent all this time, but in response

to various winks, nods, and nudges, he rose to his feet. Now, in prospect of Oiel Verree I had written the old man a brand new carol. It was a mighty achievement in the sentimental vein. I can remember only one of its couplets:

> Hold your souls in still communion,
> Blend them in a holy union.

I am not very sure what this may mean, and Billy must have been in the same uncertainty. Shall I ever forget what happened? Billy standing in the pew with my paper in his hand the wrong way up. Myself by his side holding a candle to him. Then he began to sing. It was an awful tune—I think he called it sevens—but he made common-sense of my doggerel by one alarming emendation. When he came to the couplet I have given you, what do you think he sang?

> "Hold your souls in still communion,
> Blend them in—a hollow onion!"

Billy must have been a humorist. He is long dead, poor old Billy. God rest him!

DECAY OF THE MANX LANGUAGE

If in this unscientific way I have conveyed my idea of Manx carvals, Manx ballads, or Manx proverbs, you will not be surprised to hear me say that I do not think that any of these can live long apart from the Manx language. We may have stolen most of them; they may have been wrecked on our coast, and we may have smuggled them; but as long as they wear our native homespun clothes they are ours, and as soon as they put it off they cease to belong to us. A Manx proverb

is no longer a Manx proverb when it is in English. The same
is true of a Manx ballad translated, and of a Manx carval
turned into an English carol. What belongs to us, our way of
saying things, in a word, our style, is gone. The spirit is
departed, and that which remains is only an English ghost
flitting about in Manx grave-clothes.

Now this is a sad fact, for it implies that little as we have
got of Manx literature, whether written or oral, we shall soon
have none at all. Our Manx language is fast dying out. If we
had any great work in the Manx tongue, that work alone
would serve to give our language a literary life at least. But
we have no such great work, no fine Manx poem, no good
novel in Manx, not even a Manx sermon of high mark. Thus
far our Manx language has kept alive our pigmies of Manx
literature; but both are going down together. The Manx is not
much spoken now. In the remoter villages, like Cregnesh,
Ballaugh, Kirk Michael, and Kirk Andreas, it may still be
heard. Moreover, the Manxman may hear Manx a hundred
times for every time an Englishman hears it. But the younger
generation of Manx folk do not speak Manx, and very often
do not understand it. This is a rapid change on the condition
of things in my own boyhood. Manx is to me, for all practical
uses, an unknown tongue. I cannot speak it, I cannot follow
it when spoken, I have only a sort of nodding acquaintance
with it out of door, and yet among my earliest recollections
is that of a household where nothing but Manx was ever
spoken except to me. A very old woman, almost bent double
over a spinning wheel, and calling me Hommy-Veg, and
baugh-millish, and so forth. This will suggest that the Manx
people are themselves responsible for the death of the Manx
language. That is partly true. The Manx tongue was felt to be
an impediment to intercourse with the English people. Then
the great English immigration set in, and the Isle of Man
became a holiday resort. That was the doomster of the Manx

language. In another five-and-twenty years the Manx language will be as dead as a Manx herring.

One cannot but regret this certain fate. I dare not say that the language itself is so good that it ought to live. Those who know it better say that "it's a fine old tongue, rich and musical, full of meaning and expression."* I know that it is at least forcible, and loud and deep in sound. I will engage two Manxmen quarrelling in Manx to make more noise in a given time than any other two human brethren in Christendom, not excepting two Irishmen. Also I think the Manx must be capable of notes of sweet feeling, and I observe that a certain higher lilt in a Manx woman's voice, suggesting the effort to speak about the sound of the sea, and the whistle of the wind in the gorse, is lost in the voices of the younger women who speak English only. But apart from tangible loss, I regret the death of the Manx tongue on grounds of sentiment. In this old tongue our fathers played as children, bought and sold as men, prayed, preached, gossiped, quarrelled, and made love. It was their language at Tynwald; they sang their grim carvals in it, and their wailing, woeful ballads. When it is dead more than half of all that makes us Manxmen will be gone. Our individuality will be lost, the greater barrier that separates us from other peoples will be broken down. Perhaps this may have its advantages, but surely it is not altogether a base desire not to be submerged into all the races of the earth. The tower of Babel is built, the tongues of the builders are confounded, and we are not all anxious to go back and join the happy family that lived in one ark.

But aside from all lighter thoughts there is something very moving and pathetic in the death of an old language. Permit me to tell you, not as a philologist, a character to which I have no claim, but as an imaginative writer, how the death of an

* *The Rev. T. E. Brown.*

ancient tongue affects me. It is unlike any other form of death, for an unwritten language is even as a breath of air which when it is spent leaves no trace behind. A nation may die, yet its history remains, and that is the tangible part of its past. A city may fall to decay and lie a thousand years under the sands of the desert, yet its relics revivify its life. But a language that is dead, a tongue that has no life in its literature, is a breath of wind that is gone. A little while and it went from lip to lip, from lip to ear; it came we know not whence; it has passed we know not where. It was an embodied spirit of all man's joys and sorrows, and like a spirit it has vanished away.

Then if this old language has been that of our own people its death is a loss to our affections. Indeed, language gets so close to our heart that we can hardly separate it from our emotions. If you do not speak the Italian language, ask yourself whether Dante comes as close to you as Shakespeare, all questions of genius and temperament apart. And if Dante seems a thousand miles away, and Shakespeare enters into your closest chamber, is it not first of all because the language of Shakespeare is your own language, alive with the life that is in your own tongue, vital with your own ways of thought and even tricks and whims of speech? Let English die, and Shakespeare goes out of your closet, and passes away from you, and is then your brother-Englishman only in name. So close is the bond of language, so sweet and so mysterious.

But there is yet a more sacred bond with the language of our fathers when it can have no posthumous life in books. This is the bond of love. Think what it is that you miss first and longest when death robs you of a friend. Is it not the living voice? The living face you can bring back in memory, and in your dark hours it will shine on you still; the good deed can never die; the noble thought lives for ever. Death is not conqueror over such as these, but the human voice, the strange and beautiful part of us that is half spirit in life, is lost in death. For a while it startles us as an echo in an empty chamber, and then it is gone, and not all the world's wealth could bring one note of it back. And such as the vanishing away of the voice of the friend we loved is the death of the old tongue which our fathers spoke. *It is the death of the dead.*

MANX SUPERSTITIONS

When the Manx tongue is dead there will remain, however, just one badge of our race—our superstition. I am proud to tell you that we are the most superstitious people now left among the civilised nations of the world. This is a distinction in these days when that poetry of life, as Goethe names it, is all but gone from the face of the earth. Manxmen have not yet taken the poetry out of the moon and the stars, and the mist of the mountains and the wail of the sea. Of course we are ashamed of the survival of our old beliefs and try to hide them, but let nobody say that as a people we believe no longer in charms, and the evil eye, and good spirits and bad. I know we do. It would be easy to give you a hundred illustrations. I remember an ill-tempered old body living on the Curragh, who was supposed to possess the evil eye. If a cow died at calving, she had witched it. If a baby cried suddenly in its sleep, the old witch must have been going by on the road. If the potatoes were blighted, she had looked over the hedge at them. There was a charm doctor in Kirk Andreas, named Teare-Ballawhane. He was before my time, but I recall many stories of him. When a cow was sick of the witching of the woman of the Curragh, the farmer fled over to Kirk Andreas for the charm of the charm-doctor. From the moment Teare-Ballawhane began to boil his herbs the cow recovered. If the cow died after all, there was some fault in the farmer. I remember a child, a girl, who twenty years ago had a birthmark on her face—a broad red stain like a hand on her cheek. Not long since, I saw her as a young woman, and the stain was either gone entirely or hidden by her florid complexion. When I asked what had been done for her, I heard that a good woman had charmed her. "Aw, yes," said the girl's mother, "a few good words do no harm anyway." Not long ago I met an old fellow in Onchan village who believed in the Nightman, an evil spirit who haunts the mountains at night predicting tempests and the doom of ships, the *dooinney-oie* of the Manx, akin to the *banshee* of the Irish. "Aw, man," said he, "it was up Snaefell way, and I was coming from Kirk Michael over, and it was black dark, and I heard the Nightman after me, shoutin' and wailin' morthal, *how-la-a, how-a-a*. But I didn't do nothin', no, and he came up to me lek a besom, and went past me same as a flood, *who-o-o*! And I lerr him! Aw, yes, man, yes!"

I remember many a story of fairies, some recited half in humour, others in grim earnest. One old body told me that on the night of her wedding-day, coming home from the Curragh, whither she had stolen away in pursuit of a belated calf, she was chased in the moonlight by a troop of fairies. They held on to her gown, and climbed on her back, and perched on her shoulders, and clung to her hair. There were "hundreds and tons" of them; they were about as tall as a wooden broth-ladle, and all wore cocked-hats and velvet jackets.

A good fairy long inhabited the Isle of Man. He was called in Manx the Phynnodderee. It would appear that he had two brothers of like features with himself, one in Scotland called the Brownie, the other in Scandinavia called the Swartalfar. I have often heard how on a bad night the Manx folk would go off to bed early so that the Phynnodderee might come in out of the cold. Before going upstairs they built up the fire, and set the kitchen table with crocks of milk and pecks of oaten cake for the entertainment of their guest. Then while they slept the Phynodderee feasted, yet he always left the table exactly as he found it, eating the cake and drinking the milk, but filling up the peck and the crock afresh. Nobody ever intruded upon him, so nobody ever saw him, save the Manx Peeping Tom. I remember hearing an old Manxman say that his curiosity overcame his reverence, and he "leff the wife," stepped out of bed, crept to the head of the stairs, and peeped over the banisters into the kitchen. There he saw the Phynnodderee sitting in his own arm-chair, with a great company of brother and sister fairies about him, baking bread on the griddle, and chattering together like linnets in spring. But he could not understand a word they were saying.

I have told you that the Manxman is not built by nature for a gallant. He has one bad fairy, and she is the embodied spirit of a beautiful woman. Manx folk-lore, like Manx carvals, Manx ballads, and Manx proverbs, takes it for a bad sign of a woman's character that she has personal beauty. If she is beautiful, ten to one she is a witch. That is how it happens that there are so many witches in the Isle of Man.

The story goes that a beautiful wicked witch entrapped the men of the island. They would follow her anywhere. So she led them into the sea, and they were all drowned. Then the women of the island went forth to punish her, and, to escape from them, she took the form of a wren and flew away. That is how it comes about that the poor little wren is hunted and killed on St. Stephen's Day. The Manx lads do it, though surely it ought to be the Manx maidens. At midnight they sally forth in great companies, armed with sticks and carrying torches. They beat the hedges until they light on a wren's nest, and, having started the wren and slaughtered it, they suspend the tiny mite to the middle of a long pole, which is borne by two lads from shoulder to shoulder. They then sing a rollicking native ditty, of which one version runs:—

We'll hunt the wren, says Robbin the Bobbin;
We'll hunt the wren, says Richard the Robbin;
We'll hunt the wren, says Jack of the Lan';
We'll hunt the wren, says every one.

But Robbin the Bobbin and Richard the Robbin are not the only creatures who have disappeared into the sea. The fairies themselves have also gone there. They inhabit Man no more. A Wesleyan preacher declared some years ago that he witnessed the departure of all the Manx fairies from the Bay of Douglas. They went away in empty rum puncheons, and scudded before the wind as far as the eye could reach, in the direction of Jamaica. So we have done with them, both good and bad.

However, among the witches whom we have left to us in remote corners of the island is the very harmless one called the Queen of the Mheillia. Her rural Majesty is a sort of first cousin of the Queen of the May. The Mheillia is the harvest-home. It is a picturesque ceremonial, observed differently in different parts. Women and girls follow the reapers to gather and bind the corn after it has fallen to the swish of the sickles. A handful of the standing corn of the last of the farmer's fields is tied about with ribbon. Nobody but the farmer knows where that handful is, and the girl who comes upon it by chance is made the Queen of the Mheillia. She takes it to the highest eminence near, and waves it, and her fellow-reapers and gleaners shout huzzars. Their voices are heard through the valley, where other farmers and other reapers and gleaners stop in their work and say, "So-and-so's Mheillia!" "Ballamona's Mheillia's took!" That night the farmer gives a feast in his barn to celebrate the getting in of his harvest, and the close of the work of the women at the harvesting. Sheep's heads for a change on Manx herrings, English ale for a change on Manx jough; then dancing led by the mistress, to the tune of a fiddle, played faster and wilder as the night advances, reel and jig, jig and reel. This pretty rural festival is still observed, though it has lost much of its quaintness. I think I can just remember to have heard the shouts of the Mheillia from the breasts of the mountains.

You will have gathered that in no part of the world could you find a more reckless and ill-conditioned breeding-ground of suppositions, legends, traditions, and superstitions than in the Isle of Man. The custom of hunting the wren is widely spread throughout Ireland; and if I were to tell you of Manx wedding customs, Manx burial customs, Manx birth customs. May day, Lammas, Good Friday, New Year, and Christmas customs, you would recognise in the Manxman the same irresponsible tendency to appropriate whatever flotsam drifts to his shore. What I have told you has come mainly of my own observation, but for a complete picture of Manx manners and customs, beliefs and superstitions, I will refer you to William Kennish's "Mona's Isle, and other Poems," a rare book, with next to no poetic quality, and containing much that is worthless, but having a good body of real native stuff in it, such as cannot be found elsewhere. A still better anthology is likely to be soon forthcoming from the pen of Mr. A. W. Moore (the excellent editor of "Manx Names") and the press of Mr. Nutt.

It is easy to laugh at these old superstitions, so childish do they seem, so foolish, so ignorant. But shall we therefore set ourselves so much above our fathers because they were slaves to them, and we believe them not? Bethink you. Are we so much wiser, after all? How much farther have we got? We know the mists of Mannanan. They are only the vapours from the south, creeping along the ridge of our mountains, going north. Is that enough to know? We know the cold eye of the evil man, whose mere presence hurts us, and the warm eye of the born physician, whose mere presence heals us. Does that tell us everything? We hear the moans which the sea sends up to the mountains, when storms are coming, and ships are to be wrecked, and we do not call them the voices of the Nightman, but only the voices of the wind. We have changed the name; but we have taken none of the mystery and marvel out of the thing itself. It is the Wind for us; it was the Nightman for our fathers. That is nearly all. The wind bloweth where it listeth. We are as far off as ever. Our superstitions remain, only we call them Science, and try not to be afraid of them. But we are as little children after all, and the best of us are those that, being wisest, see plainest that, before the wonders and terrors of the great world we live in, we are children, walking hand-in-hand in fear.

MANX STORIES

You will say that there ought to be many good stories of a people like the Manx; and here again I have to confess to you that the absence of all literary conscience, all perception of keeping and relation, all sense of harmony and congruity in the Manxman has so demoralised our anecdotal *ana* that I hesitate to offer you certain of the best of our Manx yarns from fear that they may be venerable English, Irish, and. Scotch familiars. I will content myself with a few that bear undoubted Manx lineaments. As an instance of Manx hospitality, simple and rude, but real and hearty, I think you would go the world over to match this. The late Rev. Hugh Stowell Brown, a Manxman, brother of the most famous of living Manxmen, and himself our North-country Spurgeon, with his wife, his sister, and his mother, were belated one evening up Baldwin Glen, and stopped at a farmhouse to inquire their way. But the farmer would not hear of their going a step further. "Aw, nonsense!" he said. "What's the use

of talkin', man? You'll be stoppin' with us to-night. Aw 'deed
ye will, though. The women can get along together aisy, and
you're a clane lookin' sort o' chap; you'll be sleepin' with me."

In the old days of, say, two steamboats a week to England
the old Manx captains of the Steamboat Company were
notorious soakers. There is a story of one of them who had
the Archdeacon of the island aboard in a storm. It was night.
The reverend Archdeacon was in an agony of pain and terror.
He inquired anxiously of the weather. The captain, very
drunk, answered, "If it doesn't mend we'll all be in heaven
before morning, Archdeacon!" "Oh, God forbid, captain,"
cried the Archdeacon.

I have said what true work for religion Nonconformity
must have done in those evil days when the clergy of the
Athols were more busy with backgammon than with
theology. But the religion of the old type of Manx Methodist
was often an amusing mixture of puritanism and its
opposite, a sort of grim, white-faced sanctity, that was never
altogether free of the suspicion of a big boisterous laugh
behind it. The Methodist local preachers have been the real
guardians and repositories of one side of the Manx genius, a
curious, hybrid thing, deadly earnest, often howlingly
ludicrous, simple, generally sincere, here and there
audaciously hypocritical. Among local preachers I
remember some of the sweetest, purest, truest men that ever
walked this world of God; but I also remember a man who
was brought home from market on Saturday night, dead
drunk, across the bottom of his cart drawn by his faithful
horse, and I saw him in the pulpit next morning, and heard
his sermon on the evils of backsliding. There is a story of the
jealousy of two local preachers. The one went to hear the
other preach. The preacher laid out his subject under a great
many heads, firstly, secondly, thirdly, up to tenthly. His rival
down below in the pew spat and *haw'd* and *tchut'd* a good

deal, and at last, quite impatient of getting no solid religious food, cried aloud, "Give us mate, man, give us mate!" Whereupon the preacher leaned over the pulpit cushion, and said, "Hould on, man, till I've done with the carving."

But to tell of Happy Dan, and his wondrous sermon on the Prodigal Son at the Clover Stones, Lonan, and his discourse on the swine possessed of devils who went "triddle-traddle, triddle-traddle down the brews and were dane drownded;" and of the marvellous account of how King David remonstrated in broadest Manx *patois* with the "pozzle-tree" for being blown down; and then of the grim earnestness of a good man who could never preach on a certain text without getting wet through to the waistcoat with perspiration—to open the flood-gates of this kind of Manx story would be to liberate a reservoir that would hardly know an end, so I must spare you.

MANX "CHARACTERS"

At various points of my narrative I have touched on certain of our eccentric Manx "characters." But perhaps more interesting than any such whom I have myself met with are some whom I have known only by repute. These children of Nature are after all the truest touchstones of a nation's genius. Crooked, distorted, deformed, they nevertheless, and perhaps therefore, show clearly the bent of their race. If you are without brake or curb you may be blind, but you must know when you are going down hill. The curb of education, and the brake of common-sense are the surest checks on a people's individuality. And these poor halfwits of the Manx race, wiser withal than many of the Malvolios who smile on them so demurely, exhibit the two great racial qualities of the Manx people—the Celtic and the Norse—

in vivid companionship and contrast. It is an amusing fact that in some wild way the bardic spirit breaks out in all of them. They are all singers, either of their own songs, or the songs of others. That surely is the Celtic strain in them. But their songs are never of the joys of earth or of love, or yet of war; never, like the rustic poetry of the Scotch, full of pawky humour; never cynical, never sarcastic; only concerned with the terrors of judgment and damnation and the place of torment. That, also, may be a fierce and dark development of the Celtic strain, but I see more of the Norse spirit in it. When my ancient bard in Glen Rushen took down his thumb-marked, greasy, discoloured poems from the "lath" against the open-timbered ceiling, and read them aloud to me in his broad Manx dialect, with a sing-song of voice and a swinging motion of body, while the loud hailstorm pelted the window pane and the wind whistled round the house, I found they were all startling and almost ghastly appeals to the sinner to shun his evil courses. One of them ran like this;

HELL IS HOT.

O sinner, see your dangerous state,
And think of hell ere 'tis too late;
When worldly cares would drown each thought,
Pray call to mind that hell is hot.
Still to increase your godly fears,
Let this be sounding in your ears,
Still bear in mind that hell is hot,
Remember and forget it not.

There was another poem about a congregation of the dead in the region of the damned:

I found a reverend parson there,
　　A congregation too,
Bowed on their bended knees at prayer,
　　As they were wont to do.
But soon my heart was struck with pain,
　　I thought it truly odd,
The parson's prayer did not contain
　　A word concerning God.

You will remember the Danish book called "Letters from Hell," containing exactly the same idea, and conclude that the Manx bard was poking fun at some fashionable yet worldly-minded preacher. But no; he was too much a child of Nature for that.

There is not much satire in the Manx character, and next to no cynicism at all. The true Manxman is white-hot. I have heard of one, John Gale, called the Manx Burns, who lampooned the upstarts about him, and also of one, Tom the Dipper, an itinerant Manx bard, who sang at fairs; but in a general way the Manx bard has been a deadly earnest person, most at home in churchyards. There was one such, akin in character to my old friend Billy of Maughold, but of more universal popularity, a quite privileged pet of everybody, a sort of sacred being, though as crazy as man may be, called Chalse-a-Killey. Chaise was scarcely a bard, but a singer of the songs of bards. He was a religious monomaniac, who lived before his time, poor fellow; his madness would not be seen in him now. The idol of his crazed heart was Bishop Wilson. He called him *dear* and *sweet*, vowed he longed to die, just that he might meet him in heaven; then Wilson would take him by the hand, and he would tell him all his mind, and together they would set up a printing press, with the types of diamonds, and print hymns, and send them back to the Isle of Man. Poor, 'wildered brain, haunted by "half-born thoughts," not all delusions, but quaint and grotesque. Full of valiant fury, Chaise was always ready to fight for his distorted phantom of the right. When an uncle of my own died, whose name I bear, Chaise shocked all the proprieties by announcing his intention of walking in front of the funeral procession through the streets and singing his terrible hymns. He would yield to no persuasion, no appeals, and no threats. He had promised the dead man that he would do this, and he would not break his oath to save his life. It was agony to the mourners, but they had to submit. Chaise fulfilled his vow, walked ten yards in front, sang his fierce music with the tears streaming from his wild eyes down his quivering face. But the spectacle let loose no unseemly mirth. Nobody laughed, and surely if the heaven that Chaise feared was listening and looking down, his crazy voice was not the last to pierce the dome of it. My friend the Rev. T. E. Brown has written a touching and beautiful poem, "To Chaise in Heaven":

> So you are gone, dear Chaise!
> Ah well; it was enough—
> The ways were cold, the ways were rough.
> O Heaven! O home!
> No more to roam,
>   Chaise, poor Chaise!
> And now it's all so plain, dear Chaise!
>   So plain—
>   The 'wildered brain
>   The joy, the pain
> The phantom shapes that haunted,
> The half-born thoughts that daunted:
>   All, all is plain,
>   Dear Chaise!
> All is plain.

Ah now, dear Chaise! of all the radiant host,
Who loves you most?
I think I know him, kneeling on his knees;
Is it Saint Francis of Assise?
     Chaise, poor Chaise.

MANX CHARACTERISTICS

I have rambled on too long about my eccentric Manx characters, and left myself little space for a summary of the soberer Manx characteristics. These are independence, modesty, a degree of sloth, a non-sanguine temperament, pride, and some covetousness. This uncanny combination of characteristics is perhaps due to our mixed Celtic and Norse blood. Our independence is pure Norse. I have never met the like of it, except in Norway, where a Bergen policeman who had hunted all the morning for my lost umbrella would not take anything for his pains; and in Iceland, where a poor old woman in a ragged woollen dress, a torn hufa on her head, torn skin shoes on her feet, and with rheumatism playing visible havoc all over her body, refused a kroner with the dignity, grave look, stiffened lips, and proud head that would have become a duchess. But the Manxman's independence almost reaches a vice. He is so unwilling to owe anything to any man that he is apt to become self-centred and cold, and to lose one of the sweetest joys of life—that of receiving great favours from those we greatly love, between whom and ourselves there is no such thing as an obligation, and no such thing as a debt. There is something in the Manxman's blood that makes him hate rank; and though he has a vast respect for wealth, it must be his own, for he will take off his hat to nobody else's.

The modesty of the Manxman reaches shyness, and his

shyness is capable of making him downright rude. One of my friends tells a charming story, very characteristic of our people, of a conversation with the men of the herring-fleet. "We were comin' home from the Shetland fishing, ten boats of us; and we come to an anchor in a bay. And there was a tremenjis fine castle there, and a ter'ble great lady. Aw, she was a ter'ble kind lady; she axed the lot of us (eighty men and boys, eight to each boat) to come up and have dinner with Her. So the day come—well, none of us went! That shy!" My friend reproved them soundly, and said he wished he knew who the lady was that he might write to her and apologise. Then followed a long story of how a breeze sprung up and eight of the boats sailed. After that the crew of the remaining two boats, sixteen men and boys, went up to the tremenjis great castle, and the ter'ble great lady, and had tea. If any lady here present knows a lady on the north-west coast of Scotland who a year or two back invited eighty Manx men and boys to dinner, and received sixteen to tea, she will redeem the character of our race if she will explain that it was not because her hospitality was not appreciated that it was not accepted by our foolish countrymen!

There is nothing that more broadly indicates the Norse strain in the Manx character than the nonsanguine temperament of the Manxmen. Where the pure Celt will hope anything and promise everything, the Manxman will hope not at all and promise nothing. "Middling" is the commonest word in a Manxman's mouth. Hardly anything is entirely good, or wholly bad, but nearly everything is middling. It's a middling fine day, or a middling stormy one; the sea is middling smooth or middling rough; the herring harvest is middling big or middling little; a man is never much more than middling tired, or middling well, or middling hungry, or middling thirsty, and the place you are travelling to is always middling near or middling far. The true

Manxman commits himself to nothing. When Nelson was shot down at Trafalgar, Cowle, a one-armed Manx quartermaster, caught him in his remaining arm. This was Cowle's story: "He fell right into my arms, sir. 'Mr. Cowle,' he says, 'do you think I shall recover?' 'I think, my lord,' I says, 'we had better wait for the opinion of the medical man.'" Dear old Cowle, that cautious word showed you were no Irishman, but a downright middling Manxman.

I have one more story to tell, and that is of Manx pride, which is a wondrous thing, usually very ludicrous. A young farming girl who will go about barefoot throughout the workdays of the week would rather perish than not dress in grand attire, after her own sort, on Sunday afternoon. But Manx pride in dress can be very touching and human. When the lighthouse was built on the Chickens Rock, the men who were to live in it were transferred from two old lighthouses on the little islet called the Calf of Man, but their families were left in the disused lighthouses. Thus the men were parted from their wives and children, but each could see the house of the other, and on Sunday mornings the wives in their old lighthouses always washed and dressed the children and made them "nice" and paraded them to and fro on the platforms in front of the doors, and the men in their new lighthouse always looked across the Sound at their little ones through their powerful telescopes.

MANX TYPES

Surely that is a lovely story, full of real sweetness and pathos. It reminds me that amid many half-types of dubious quality, selfish, covetous, quarrelsome, litigious, there are at least two types of Manx character entirely charming and delightful. The one is the best type of Manx seaman, a true son of the sea, full of wise saws and proverbs, full of long yarns and wondrous adventures, up to anything, down to anything, pragmatical, a mighty moralist in his way, but none the less equal to a round ringing oath; a sapient adviser putting on the airs of a philosopher, but as simple as the baby of a girl—in a word, dear old Tom Baynes of "Fo'c's'le Yarns," old salt, old friend, old rip. The other type is that of the Manx parish patriarch. This good soul it would be hard to beat among all the peoples of earth. He unites the best qualities of both sexes; he is as soft and gentle as a dear old woman, and as firm of purpose as a strong man. Garrulous, full of platitudes, easily moved to tears by a story of sorrow and as easily taken in, but beloved and trusted and reverenced by all the little world about him. I have known him as a farmer, and seen him sitting at the head of his table in the farm kitchen, with his sons and daughters and men-servants and women-servants about him, and, save for ribald gossip, no one of whatever condition abridged the flow of talk for his presence. I have known him as a parson, when he has been the father of his parish, the patriarch of his people, the "ould angel" of all the hillside round about. Such sweetness in his home life, such nobility, such gentle, old-fashioned ceremoniousness, such delightful simplicity of manners. Then when two of these "ould angels" met, two of these Parson Adamses, living in content on seventy pounds a year, such high talk on great themes, long hour after long hour in the little low-ceiled Vicarage study, with no light but the wood fire, which glistened on the diamond window-pane! And when midnight came seeing each other home, spending half the night walking to and fro from Vicarage to Vicarage, or turning out to saddle the horse in the field, but (far away "in wandering mazes lost") going blandly up to the old cow and putting on the blinkers and saying, "Here he is, sir." Have we anything like all this in England? Their type is nearly extinct even in the Isle of Man, where they have longest survived. And indeed they are not the only good things that are dying out there.

LITERARY ASSOCIATIONS

The island has next to no literary associations, but it would be unpardonable in a man of letters if he were to forget the few it can boast. Joseph Train, our historian, made the acquaintance of Scott in 1814, and during the eighteen years following he rendered important services to "The Great Unknown" as a collector of some of the legendary stories used as foundations for what were then called the Scotch Novels. But it is a common error that Train found the groundwork of the Manx part of "Peveril of the Peak." It was Scott who directed Train to the Isle of Man as a fine subject for study. Scott's brother Thomas lived there, and no doubt this was the origin of Scott's interest in the island. Scott himself never set foot on it. Wordsworth visited the island about 1823, and he recorded his impressions in various sonnets, and also in the magnificent lines on Peel Castle—"I was thy neighbour once, thou rugged pile." He also had a relative living there—Miss Hutchinson, his sister-in-law. A brother of this lady, a mariner, lies buried in Braddan churchyard, and his tombstone bears an epitaph which Wordsworth indited. The poet spent a summer at Peel, pitching his tent above what is now called Peveril Terrace. One of my friends tried long ago to pump up from this sapless soil some memory of Wordsworth, but no one could remember anything about him. Shelley is another poet of whom there remains no trace in the Isle of Man. He visited the island early in 1812, being driven into Douglas harbour by contrary winds on his voyage from Cumberland to Ireland. He was then almost unknown;

Harriet was still with him, and his head was full of political reforms. The island was in a state of some turmoil, owing to the unpopularity of the Athols, who still held manorial rights and the patronage of the Bishopric. The old Norse Constitution was intact, and the House of Keys was then a self-elected chamber. It is not wonderful that Shelley made no impression on Man in 1812, but it is surprising that Man seems to have made no impression on Shelley. It made a very sensible impression on Hawthorne, who left his record in the "English Note Book."

MANX PROGRESS

I am partly conscious that throughout these lectures I have kept my face towards the past. That has been because I have been loathe to look at the present, and almost afraid to peep into the future. The Isle of Man is not now what it was even five-and-twenty years ago. It has become too English of late. The change has been sudden. Quite within my own recollection England seemed so far away that there was something beyond conception moving and impressive in the effect of it and its people upon the imagination of the Manx. There were only about two steamers a week between England and the Isle of Man at that time. Now there are about two a day. There are lines of railway on this little plot of land, which you might cross on foot between breakfast and lunch, and cover from end to end in a good day's walk. This is, of course, a necessity of the altered conditions, as also, no doubt, are the parades, and esplanades, and promenades, and iron piers, and marine carriage drives, and Eiffel Tower, and old castles turned into Vauxhall Gardens, and fairy glens into "happy day" Roshervilles. God forbid that I should grudge the factory hand his breath of the sea and glimpse of the gorse-bushes; but I know what price we are paying that we may entertain him.

Our young Manxman is already feeling the English immigration on his character. He is not as good a man as his father was before him. I dare say that in his desire to make everything English that is Manx, he may some day try to abolish the House of Keys, or at least dig up the Tynwald Hill. In one fit of intermittent mania, he has already attempted to "restore" the grand ruins of Peel Castle, getting stones from Whitehaven, filling up loop-holes, and doing other indecencies with the great works of the dead. All this could be understood if the young Manxman were likely to be much the richer for the changes he is bringing about. But he is not; the money that comes from England is largely taken by English people, and comes back to England.

CONCLUSION

From these ungracious thoughts let me turn again, in a last word, to the old island itself, the true Mannin-veg-Veen of the real Manxman. In these lectures you have seen it only as in flashes from a dark lantern. I am conscious that an historian would have told you so much more of solid fact that you might have carried away tangible ideas. Fact is not my domain, and I shall have to be content if in default of it I have got you close to that less palpable thing, the living heart of Manxland, shown you our island, helped you to see its blue waters and to scent its golden gorse, and to know the Manxman from other men. Sometimes I have been half ashamed to ask you to look at our countrymen, so rude are they and so primitive—russet-coated, currane-shod men and women, untaught, superstitious, fishing the sea, tilling their stony land, playing next to no part in the world, and only gazing out on it as a mystery far away, whereof the rumour comes over the great waters. No great man among us, no great event in our history, nothing to make us memorable. But I have been re-assured when I have remembered that, after all, to look on a life so simple and natural might even be a tonic. Here we are in the heart of the mighty world, which the true Manxman knows only by vague report; millions on millions huddled together, enough to make five hundred Isles of Man, more than all the Manxmen that have lived since the days of Orry, more than all that now walk on the island, added to all that rest under it; streets on streets of us, parks on parks, living a life that has no touch of Nature in the ways of it; save only in our own breasts, which often rebel against our surroundings, struggling with weariness under their artificiality, and the wild travesty of what we are made for. Do what we will, and be what we may, sometimes we feel the falseness of our ways of life, and surely it is then a good and wholesome thing to go back in thought to such children of Nature as my homespun Manx people, and see them where Nature placed them, breathing the free air of God's proper world, and living the right lives of His servants, though so simple, poor, and rude.

END